ASPECTS OF REASON

Aspects of Reason

PAUL GRICE

With an introduction by
Richard Warner

CLARENDON PRESS · OXFORD
2001

OXFORD

UNIVERSITY PRESS

Great Clarendon Street, Oxford OX2 6DP

Oxford University Press is a department of the University of Oxford.
It furthers the University's objective of excellence in research, scholarship,
and education by publishing worldwide in

Oxford New York

Athens Auckland Bangkok Bogotá Buenos Aires
Cape Town Chennai Dar es Salaam Delhi Florence Hong Kong Istanbul
Karachi Kolkata Kuala Lumpur Madrid Melbourne Mexico City Mumbai
Nairobi Paris São Paulo Shanghai Singapore Taipei Tokyo Toronto Warsaw

and associated companies in Berlin Ibadan

Oxford is a registered trade mark of Oxford University Press
in the UK and certain other countries

Published in the United States
by Oxford University Press Inc., New York

British Library Cataloguing in Publication Data

Data available

Library of Congress Cataloging in Publication Data
Grice, H. P. (H. Paul)
Aspects of reason/Paul Grice ; with an introduction by Richard Warner.
p. cm.
Includes bibliographical references and index.
1. Reasoning. I. Title.
B1641.G483 A86 2001 128'.33—dc21 2001016403
ISBN 0–19–824252–2

1 3 5 7 9 10 8 6 4 2

Typeset by Graphicraft Limited, Hong Kong
Printed in Great Britain by
Biddles Ltd., Guildford & King's Lynn

CONTENTS

INTRODUCTION

Grice on Reasons and Rationality

RICHARD WARNER

Paul Grice opens *Aspects of Reason* by observing that

more than one philosopher has held the view that vitally important philosophical consequences can be reached by derivation from the idea of a rational being. Aristotle, for example, thought that he could reach a characterization of the end for man ... And Kant considered that among the important dividends which could be derived from the idea of a rational being was the moral necessity of adherence to the Categorical Imperative. (4)[1]

Grice does not "know whether or not any such grand conclusions can be derived from the concept of a rational being", but he confesses to a "sneaking hope that they can, and a nagging desire to try to find out" (4). The hope and the desire motivate *Aspects of Reason*, a work in which Grice conceives of himself as an "underlabourer [engaging] in one or two enquiries which might help towards a clarification of the notion of reason or rationality" (5). Clarification is required for the task of reaching "vitally important philosophical consequences ... by derivation from the idea of a rational being" (4). Grice explains: "Part of my trouble (which is not only mine) is the difficulty of discovering the rules of the game, of understanding what sort of procedure is to be counted as a derivation; another part of my trouble is being hopelessly unclear about the character of the starting point, about what the concept of a rational being is to be taken to be" (4). Most of *Aspects of Reason* is concerned with the "starting point", the concept of rationality, although there are side glances towards what might count as a derivation of consequence from that concept.

---

[1] Numbers in parentheses refer to pages in the text of *Aspects of Reason*.

Grice worked on *Aspects of Reason* on and off from (at least) 1975 up to the end of his life in 1988; nonetheless, *Aspects of Reason* remains an unfinished work, lacking the clean conceptual unity of Grice's published works. The original manuscript consists of a basic set of typed pages interleaved with lengthy (often hand-written) augmentations added at different times.[2] The result is a book of rewarding richness and detail, but also one whose unity and overall plan are difficult to discern. As its title suggests, *Aspects of Reason* looks more like a tour through a varied landscape than a precise portrait of a well-defined terrain; its five chapters look, at first sight, less like a book and more like five loosely related essays. It is, however, both possible and rewarding to see *Aspects of Reason* as a unified work, and my goal is to map out the unifying themes in the intricate conceptual landscape Grice traverses. Perhaps Grice, should he be looking down from one of the more rollicking parts of some philosophical Elysium, will not mind terribly if I suggest a few finishing touches along the way.

Chapter 4, "Practical and Alethic Reasons: Part II", holds the key to seeing *Aspects of Reason* as a unified work. That chapter contains the pivotal development of themes introduced in Chapter 3. The conclusions of Chapter 4 provide the initial motivation for Chapter 5, in which Grice begins to turn away from his role as "under-labourer" towards the project of deriving philosophical consequences from the idea of a rational being. Chapters 1 and 2 fit into this pattern, offering a discussion of reasons and reasoning crucial to defending the central thesis of Chapter 4. This is *one* way to see *Aspects of Reason* as a unified work; I hope others will propose others. Its rich terrain rewards surveying efforts.

A final preliminary issue is the connection between *Aspects of Reason* and the rest of Grice's work. The two may seem oddly disconnected. Grice does not discuss reasoning at any length elsewhere, nor does his work seem to rely on any controversial assumptions about reason and reasoning. The latter supposition would be incorrect, however. Views about reasons and reasoning underlie his theory of meaning as well as his general methodology for approaching philosophical problems.

---

[2] The two main additions occur in Chapter 2: the discussion of flat and variable rationality, and the discussion of relativized and absolute modalities.

To begin with the theory of meaning, consider the original 1957 version of that theory, in "Meaning".[3] Grice offers an account of (what he will later call) utterer's meaning, the notion of meaning involved in describing someone as meaning that he was sad by uttering 'I am blue'. Grice suggests that

by uttering 'I am blue' one means that one is sad if and only if one utters 'I am blue' intending:

(1) that the audience believe that one is sad;
(2) that the audience recognize the intention described in (1);
(3) that this recognition be part of the audience's reason for believing that one is sad.

To see the idea, suppose that you stop your car at an intersection late at night. Another car flashes its lights at you. You think: "Why is she flashing lights at me? The best explanation is that she must intend me to think my lights are not on. There is no reason for her to deceive me, so my lights really must not be on." We are to imagine the light-flasher as having engaged in similar reasoning to arrive at the conclusion that she can mean that your lights are not on by flashing her lights. The explanatory power of the theory comes from seeing utterers reasoning their way to what utterances to produce, and from seeing hearers reasoning their way to a response. The point applies equally to made-up signals like light-flashings and to communication in natural language. We can imagine you—the reader—reasoning as follows with regard to the sentence immediately preceding this one: "The sentence's standard meaning in English is 'The point applies equally to made-up signals like light-flashings and to communication in natural language'; Warner would not be producing that sentence in this context unless he intended me to think that he believes the point applies equally to made-up signals like light-flashings and to communication in natural language. He has no reason to deceive me, so he must believe that."[4]

---

[3] "Meaning", *Philosophical Review*, 66 (July 1957), 377–88.
[4] Note the intended effect here is that you believe that I think so-and-so. This change is necessary as it is only in *telling* that the intended effect is that the audience believe something. Grice takes the intended effect of *asserting* to be that the audience believe that the utterer thinks something. This elaboration occurs in "Utterer's Meaning, Sentence Meaning, and Word-Meaning", *Foundations of Language*, 4 (Aug. 1968), 225–42.

The problem, of course, is that people hardly ever reason this way when communicating. You did not reason in any such way when you read the sentence, 'The point applies equally to made-up signals like light-flashings and to communication in natural language.' You read the sentence and understood—straightaway, without any intervening reasoning, without, indeed, thinking about it at all. So, what is the relation between the reasoning you *might* have engaged in and your understanding the sentence? How is there any explanatory power in the fact that, although you reached your understanding of the sentence *in some other way*, you *might* have reasoned your way to such an understanding? The question is a critical one for Grice's theory of meaning.

The relevance of the question extends well beyond the theory of meaning, for the remarks about meaning also illustrate a key feature of Grice's philosophical methodology. Given the task of providing a philosophical account of some kind of attitude or action, or some other psychological aspect of life (for example, intending to catch the 5.01 train, doing one's duty, living a happy life), Grice would ask, "How would a person explicitly reason his way to that attitude, action, or realization of that aspect in his or her life?" His great talent would yield illuminating answers that revealed the attitude, action, or aspect as rationally justified. This facet of his methodology was often noted and discussed at Berkeley during the 1970s. This worry was, of course, that people do not really reason explicitly in the way Grice would imagine. Once, when he was taken to task for this, he replied (with some exasperation), "But there must be a rational explanation!" He was committed to seeing persons as rational agents, and to seeing rational agency as, at least in part, revealed by explicit derivations of rational justifications for attitudes and actions. *Aspects of Reason* is his explanation of the link between the explicit arguments we can—but often do not—construct, and the attitudes and actions that populate our daily life.

I. Practical and Epistemic Acceptability

Grice begins Chapter 4 by remarking: "I have been, so far, in the early stages of an attempt to estimate the prospects of what I shall now rename an '*Equivocality Thesis*' with respect to certain common modals" (90). By "common modals", Grice means "certain common words like 'must', 'ought', 'should', 'necessary', etc." (67–8). The Equivocality Thesis is "a thesis, or set of theses, with respect to particular common modals, which claims that they are univocal across the practical/alethic divide, or if they are multivocal, then their multivocality appears equally on each side of the barrier" (90). For the moment, we can think of "the practical/alethic divide" as illustrated by the division of reasons into *reasons for belief* (alethic) and *reasons for action* (practical). The Equivocality Thesis makes its first appearance in Chapter 2, where Grice formulates the claim this way:

Kant insisted that it is one and the same faculty of reason which issues in alethic reasoning and practical reasoning. How one should individuate faculties and capacities is a mystery . . . so perhaps we might make things a little easier if . . . we were to ask whether the word 'reason' has the same meaning in the phrases 'alethic reason' and 'practical reason', or (alternatively) has different meanings which are related by a greater or lesser measure of analogy. (44–5)[5]

The thesis is not as narrowly linguistic as it may appear. The development of this thesis is an essential part of Grice's clarification of the concept of rationality. The first step towards understanding the thesis is to ask, what does Grice mean by "the practical/alethic divide"?

In answer, Grice notes that the justificatory reasons, "are (or are widely thought to be) divisible into practical and non-practical (alethic) reasons" (67–8), and he observes that

Most people (even philosophical people) would . . . take the view that 'reason' has a single meaning in [both practical and alethic] contexts [in, for example, 'reason to believe' and 'reason to act'] . . . But, when we move to other words which seem to be very closely connected with reason, the situation seems to change. Kant (I suspect) would have been firmly in

[5] The quoted passage actually reads, "Kant insisted that it is one and the same faculty of reason which issues in alethic reasoning and practical reasoning. How one should individuate faculties and capacities is a mystery *which is very much unfathomed, though it is not, I hope, unfathomable; so perhaps we might make things a little easier if, instead of asking whether Kant's view is correct* . . ." (emphasis added). I do not wish my omission of this material in the text to suggest that Grice was abandoning the idea of a faculty. A theory of faculties and capacities was near and dear to his heart, and the theme arises repeatedly in *Aspects of Reason*.

favour of the idea that the word 'necessary' (and its cognates) has the same meanings (or meanings) in the two sentences (1) "It is necessary for you to go to the hospital tomorrow" and (2) "It is necessary that the paper will ignite" . . . said when someone is about to put a match to the paper . . . But . . . I am certain that there are many others who would not [take this position]. . . . It is almost common form to suppose that there are (at least) two senses of the word 'ought', exhibited severally in the sentences (1) "You ought to get your hair cut" and (said several hours later, to someone else) (2) "His hair ought to be cut by now"; these are called (respectively) the practical and the epistemic 'ought'. And what of "The roof must have fallen in" and "The butler must repair the roof"?   (45)

Additional examples of the practical and epistemic 'ought' and 'must' are in order. Consider the epistemic case first. There are a variety of things I must believe insofar as I am rational. I must believe that triangles have three sides; that water freezes at 0° centigrade; and that my name is Richard Warner. In each case, belief is, in the light of the evidence, the only rational option; and, in this sense, I both *must* and *ought* to believe. Differences between 'must' and 'ought' need not worry us; it is sufficient to note that 'must' can signal the lack of any other rational option while 'ought' is often used to indicate a consideration that may be outweighed by others (although "I ought *all things considered* believe . . ." can certainly be used to express an epistemic necessity). Contrast two examples of *practical* necessity. The first: I turn down a job in a distant city— a job absolutely crucial to advancing my career—in order, in the midst of a divorce, to stay near my two-year-old daughter. I say, "I *can't* go. I *must* stay." The second: a terrorist has planted a bomb in an elementary school, the location of which we do not know. We have apprehended the terrorist, and we are certain that, if we torture him horribly, he will reveal the school's location in time to defuse the bomb. When someone suggests torture, the chief of police says, "We *can't*. We *must* find some other way." The uses of "can't" and "must" in these examples express *practical necessities*, necessities of action or inaction. As in the epistemic case, we might also express these necessities using 'ought' ("All things considered, I ought to stay"), although, as before, 'ought' has its "potentially outweighed consideration" use.

    The point to emphasize is that epistemic necessity would seem to differ greatly from practical necessity. 'I must believe' and 'I ought to believe' express requirements of rational belief. But 'I must not torture' and 'I ought not to torture' express normative requirements. It is not unreasonable to think that we are faced with two different kinds of necessity. The answer to "Why is it necessary?" is very different in the two cases. In the epistemic case, the answer is that empirical evidence compels belief in the statement that water freezes at 0°; the prohibition on torture, on the other hand, arises (presumably) from the respect we owe persons no matter what they may have done.

Despite such considerations, Grice claims that the epistemic and the practical 'ought'/'must' do not differ in meaning; or, to repeat Grice's formulation, which is at once both more general and more cautious: the Equivocality Thesis is a thesis that "with respect to particular common modals . . . claims that they are univocal across the practical/alethic divide, or if they are multivocal, then their multivocality appears equally on each side of the barrier" (90). Whether this thesis is true is, it turns out, much less important than the conceptual constructs Grice deploys in its defence. The defence reveals important features of rationality even if the Equivocality Thesis remains debatable. This is important for another reason: it is commonplace now to reject any strict distinction between the alethic and the practical, and some will find little interest in an extended defence of what they already assume to be true.

With these points in mind, let us turn to Grice's discussion of the Equivocality Thesis. Let us stick with 'ought' and 'must' as examples with the understanding that what we say is supposed to apply to a range of "common modals". The cornerstone of Grice's defence is the suggestion that we think of alethic acceptability (expressed by the "alethic" 'ought' and 'must') and practical acceptability (expressed by the "practical" 'ought' and 'must') as both instances of a general notion of *rational acceptability*. Thus: "His hair ought to (must) be cut by now" expreses a judgement—the judicative form of the general notion of acceptance; while "He ought to get his hair cut" expresses the practical, volitive form of acceptance. For an analogy, consider the way in which, in many languages, a verb's tense, voice, and so on are expressed by adding endings to a single root. On Grice's view, the epistemic and practical forms of acceptability share a common "root" and differ in the "ending".

Grice introduces some notation to explain the idea. As he explains (using for the moment 'should', another of the "common modals", instead of 'ought' or 'must'):

An initial version of the idea I want to explore is that we represent the sentences (1) "John should be recovering his health by now" and (2) "John should join AA" as having the following structures; *first*, a common "rationality" operator "Acc", to be heard as "it is reasonable that", "it is acceptable that", "it ought to be that", "it should be that", or in some other similar way; *next*, one or other of two mood-operators, which in the case of (1) are to be written as '⊢' and in the case of (2) are to be written as '!'; and finally a 'radical', to be represented by 'r' or some other lower-case letter. The structure for (1) is Acc + ⊢ + r, for (2) Acc + ! + r, with each symbol falling within the scope of its predecessor. I am thinking of a radical in pretty much the same kind of way as recent writers who have used that term (or the term 'phrastic'); I think of it as a sequence in the underlying structural representation of sentences . . .   (50)

For now, let us put aside the linguistic claim that the structure of *sentences* containing the "common modals" is correctly represented by 'Acc + ⊢ + r' or 'Acc + ! + r'. Our current focus is on the content of thought, not the structure of speech. Grice contends that, in the case at hand, "it is legitimate to apply devices, which are initially presented as structural elements underlying mode-differences expressed in *speech*, to the representation of the content of thought, and in particular of the content of *acceptance-in-thought*" (71).[6] As the first of the above two passages shows, Grice uses 'Acc' to represent "It is rationally acceptable that". Thus

Acc A

is read as "It is rationally acceptable that A", or simply "It is acceptable that" with the rationality requirement understood. He uses '⊢' to express judicative variant of acceptability. Thus:

---

[6] In the text, this sentence is actually formulated as a question, but it is a question Grice clearly answers in the affirmative. In this passage, Grice uses 'mode' for 'mood'. Grice told me that this is the result of an objection raised by Julius Moravscik during Grice's delivery of the Immanuel Kant Lectures at Stanford. Moravscik objected that Grice's use of 'mood' did not fit with the standard use of that term in linguistics, so Grice switched to 'mode'.

Acc ⊢ A,

read as, "It is acceptable that *it is the case that* p". He uses '!' to express the volitive variant of acceptability as:

Acc ! A,

read as, "It is acceptable that *let it be that* A". Or, that is almost the right reading. To see the problem, consider that Grice glosses "Let it be that I eat my hat" as "I shall (intentional) eat my hat" (59–60). As an expression of an intention, this certainly makes sense when spoken by me (for example), and "Let it be that the defendant pays the fine" makes sense spoken by a judge with the authority to impose the fine. The point is that we have to understand '! A' as implicitly relativized to an appropriate agent, where values for 'A' are restricted to those that make sense as the specification of an intention of that agent. As Grice notes, we "find in the practical area, though not in the alethic area, non-trivial examples of relativization of modalities to individual persons . . ." (57), and he is concerned that "this bodes very ill for the contention that modalities are equivocal with respect to practical and alethic discussion" (57). As his discussion makes clear, some sort of relativization is called for in the case '! A'; for our purposes, however, we need not pursue this issue.

Instead, we should ask how the notation helps us explain practical and epistemic necessities. This is far from obvious. The notation is designed to express acceptability and does not even address issues about necessity. The link between the notation and necessity comes via derivation. Grice's position is that practical and epistemic necessity are demonstrated by *deriving* the relevant statements from suitable premises. Actually deriving a practical necessity is the best way to illustrate his idea. What follows in Section II is a reconstruction—very faithful to the underlying intent—of Grice's approach; the discussion, in Section III, of what he actually says shows the need for reconstruction.

II. Deriving Practical Necessities

The example of torturing the terrorist is convenient. Suppose that the reason that we should not torture is that it violates the respect due to persons, a respect due to them no matter what the circumstances. For our purposes, it does not matter why we should not torture, or even whether it is really true that we should not. All we care about is how to get from the *assumption* that torture violates the respect due to persons to the conclusion that we must not torture the terrorist.

We begin with:

(1) Acc ! (persons are treated with respect).

This expresses our commitment to the principle that persons are to be treated with respect. The next step is:

(2) Acc ⊢ (persons are treated with respect only if we do not torture this person).

(2) expresses the judgement that we act consistently with the demand that persons should be treated with respect only if we do not torture the person in question.[7] Next we need a principle that allows us to take premisses formulated using *both* '⊢' and '!' and derive a conclusion expressed solely in terms of '!'. Grice uses "Whoever wills the end, wills the necessary and indispensable means" for this purpose. We can express this as:

(3) For any A and B, Acc (if ! A, and ⊢ (A only if B); then ! B).

To see the next step, note that (3) entails: "If Acc ! A, and Acc ⊢ (A only if B); then Acc ! B." The English rewrite makes this plain: *it is rationally acceptable that* (if ! A, and ⊢ (A only if ⊢ B); then ! B) only if: if *it is rationally acceptable that* ! A, and *it is rationally acceptable that* (⊢ A only if ⊢ B); then *it is rationally acceptable that* ! B. So:

(4) For any A and B, if Acc ! A, and Acc ⊢ (A only if B); then Acc ! B.

We could, of course, eliminate the step from (3) to (4) by simply using (4) to represent "Whoever wills the end wills the indispensable means." There are two reasons not to.

---

[7] The use of 'only if' here requires comment. It is a convenient shorthand for two different cases. In the first, "A only if B" is equivalent to "B's being the case is causally necessary for A's being the case". In the second, it is equivalent to "B realizes A". For example, to be in Warsaw, Poland, is to realize an instance of being in Poland.

First, (3) and (4) do not mean the same thing. (4) restricts "Whoever wills the end wills the indispensable means" to cases where acceptability is *rational*. (3) imposes no such restriction, and it is clear that, in our thought and action, we use the principle in the broader way that (3) expresses. Suppose, for example, I claim to will to eat a bagel, where the only way to do so is to walk out to a restaurant in sub-zero weather. There is a sense of 'will' in which I do not really will to eat a bagel if I do not also will to walk to the restaurant. This is true even if it was not rational for me to will to eat a bagel or not rational for me to judge that the weather outside was sub-zero. The second reason to prefer (3) to (4) is that, in (3), 'Acc' appears independently— not in immediate combination with '⊢' or '!'. If 'Acc' were *never* to appear independently in derivations, it would be difficult to see in what sense it denoted acceptability-in-general. 'Acc ⊢' and 'Acc !' would just be complicated ways of writing 'must' and 'ought'. Grice does indeed let 'Acc' occur independently (see the discussion on pp. xxi–xxiii). But there is a puzzle here: what does 'Acc' mean when it occurs independently? We will return to this issue.

The point to emphasize now is that, from (1), (2), and (4), it follows that:

(5) Acc ! (we do not torture this person),

which we can read as "It is rationally acceptable that let it be that we do not torture this person." These statements are *necessary* in the sense that (5) is necessary *given (1), (2), and (4)*. Assume we are certain these conditions hold; then, it would be appropriate to express the conditional necessity by saying, "We must not torture the terrorist." It is this *conditional* necessity that we should associate with the practical 'must' and 'ought'. The example of staying with my daughter makes this clear. The facts that make it necessary that I should stay with my daughter are facts about me and my commitment to my daughter. Take these conditions away and there is no necessity. As a final point, it is worth noting that, if we fully and unqualifiedly believe (5), then, insofar as we are rational, not subject to weakness of the will, we will arrive at

(6) ! we do not torture this person,

which reads, "Let it be that we do not torture this person," or more colloquially "We shall (intentional) not torture this person." (Compare Grice's discussion on pp. 62–3.)

Now we turn to a number of puzzles and objections as a way of further defending and explaining Grice's position.

The first objection: the objection is that some practical necessities are *un*conditionally necessary. After all, are not some practical necessities derivable from premisses that are themselves unconditionally necessarily true, a status the conclusion would then also inherit? But this cannot be correct—not where the conclusion enjoins an agent to perform a particular action. Driving the necessity of a particular action will require a premiss connecting ends and means, a premiss like "Acc ⊢ (persons are treated with respect only if we do not torture this person)". This premiss will not express a necessary truth as it will be a contingent fact that this particular state of affairs is one that realizes the relevant end or ends. Of course, some practical necessities may be "less" conditional than others in the sense that they depend on fewer contingent premisses. The torture example illustrates the point. One might contend—not implausibly—that fundamental moral principles—like, perhaps, "Persons should be treated with respect"—are true a priori.

Grice looks on such views with favour. He sees moral principles as part of common-sense psychology, and he assigns common-sense psychology a special status. As he explains in another work:

The psychological theory which I envisage would be deficient as a theory to explain behaviour if it did not contain provision for the interests in ascription of psychological states other than as tools for explaining and predicting behaviour, interests (for example) on the part of one creature to be able to ascribe these rather than those psychological states to another creature. Within such a theory it should be possible to derive strong motivations on the part of the creatures subject to the theory against the abandonment of the central concepts of the theory (and so the theory itself). Motivations which the creatures would (or should) regard as justified.[8]

---

[8] "Method in Philosophical Psychology: From the Banal to the Bizarre", *Proceedings and Addresses of the American Philosophical Association*, 48 (Nov. 1975), 52.

Grice sees fundamental moral principles as self-justifying elements of common-sense psychology. Of course being self-justifying is not the same as being necessary, but he clearly regards some elements of common-sense psychology as necessarily true.

In particular, he sees "Whoever wills the end wills the necessary means" as necessarily true. He suggests that the principle is in part definitive of what it means to will. He makes the same point in *Aspects of Reason*, but does so against a much more complex background, for he treats the principle as a "fundamental psychological law":

Let us suppose it to be a *fundamental* psychological law that, *ceteris paribus*, for any creature x (of a sufficiently developed kind), no matter what A and B are, *if* x wills A and judges that if A, A only as a result of B, *then* x wills B. This I take to be a proper representation of "he who wills the end, wills the indispensable means"; and in calling it a *fundamental* law I mean that is the law, or one of the laws, from which 'willing' and 'judging' derive their sense as names of concepts which explain behaviour. So, I assume, to reject it would be to *deprive* these words of their sense. (94)

This appeal to "fundamental psychological law" reflects Grice's commitment to functionalism as an approach to explicating psychological concepts. The sense in which the principle is a "law" certainly calls for clarification as he continues by arguing that

If x is a *rational* creature, since in this case his attitudes of acceptance are at least to some degree under his control (volitive or judicative assent can be *withheld* or *refused*), this law will hold for him only if the following is true:
(2) x wills (it is x's will that) (for any A, B) if x wills that A and judges that if A, A only as a result of B, then x is to will B. (95)

Evidently, the law follows from (2) and some supplementary assumptions about rationality, and this makes the law look less like a psychological law and more like some sort of conceptual truth derived from views about rationality. Grice would, in this context, almost certainly have rejected this flat-footed distinction between psychological laws and conceptual truths, but we need not go into such issues. The point is simply that he sees "Whoever wills the end wills the indispensable means" as having a non-contingent status.

The second objection: the objection is that it is by no means evident how our derivation of a practical necessity has anything to do with the Equivocality Thesis. In reply, consider a simple epistemic argument: why should I believe that my name is Richard Warner? The answer, of course, is that I have overwhelming evidence that this is true. To make the point using Grice's notation, we begin with:

(1) Acc (If ⊢ there is overwhelming evidence that my name is Richard Warner, then ⊢ my name is Richard Warner).

This entails

(2) If Acc ⊢ there is overwhelming evidence that my name is Richard Warner, then Acc ⊢ my name is Richard Warner.

So, given

(3) Acc ⊢ there is overwhelming evidence that my name is Richard Warner.

we have

(4) Acc ⊢ my name is Richard Warner.

Of course, the argument would be much more complicated if we derived (3), "Acc ⊢ there is overwhelming evidence for A", from suitable facts and principles about evidence, and Grice takes some steps in this direction when he formulates a Principle of Total Evidence, which he argues applies equally in alethic and practical arguments (pp. 80–7). However, our simple argument is sufficient for our purposes. It illustrates how we can treat epistemic necessity as conditional, just like practical necessity. Of course, just as in the practical case, there is room for argument here about the extent to which fundamental principles for assessing evidence have an a priori character, but we can put this issue aside.

The point—and the claim—is that all the "common modals" can be treated in similar ways using 'Acc', '⊢', and '!'. Carrying out this programme through a detailed analysis of the "particular common modals" would establish the Equivocality Thesis. Grice does not provide such an analysis. At most he makes the thesis plausible by showing how to think of the practical and epistemic 'ought' and 'must' as specifications of a general notion of acceptability. He does not intend to do more. He proposes it as a thesis for investigation, not as one he will fully establish.

But are the considerations he advances sufficient even to motivate the thesis? The arguments for the thesis depend on using 'Acc', '⊢', and '!' to derive practical and alethic necessities. In these derivations, 'Acc' occurs independently—not in immediate combination with '⊢' or '!'. This is essential; otherwise, as we argued earlier, 'Acc ⊢' and 'Acc !' are just complicated ways of writing 'must' and 'ought'. The problem is: what does 'Acc' mean when it occurs independently? It must denote some attitude of acceptance, but what is that attitude? Grice offers some linguistic considerations in favour of thinking such an attitude exists:

> There seems to me to be some linguistic support for this idea. . . . words like 'reason' and 'justification' operate in both the alethic and the practical domain. "There is every reason to regard him as a fool" is, semantically, not very different from "In all probability he is a fool" . . . Similar linguistic phenomena are to hand not only with respect to "justification" but also with respect to "ought" and "should". A further hint is provided by the behaviours of the phrase "it is to be expected". To say, "It is to be expected of a lawyer that he will earn $100,000 a year," though not wholly unambiguous, seems to be on one interpretation close to "A lawyer will probably earn $100,000 a year." To say, "It is to be expected of a lawyer that he earn $100,000 a year" seems, however, to be obstinately practical in sense; it is asserted . . . that it is in some way or other incumbent on a lawyer to earn that not insignificant income. *If we accept the idea that the difference between these two statements, which consists in the difference between the presence of the verb-phrase "will earn" and that of the verb-phrase "earn", is a difference of* mood, *then it looks as if a shift from alethic to practical discourse may be signalled by a shift in mood with respect to the subordinate verb.* (49–50; emphasis added)

These examples support using the mood-operators '⊢' and '!' to indicate alethic and practical inflections of a general notion of acceptability.

Grice does not, of course, see these examples as decisive. He supplements the examples with considerations drawn from his theory of meaning.[9] His account of sentence-meaning consists in specifying procedures that a speaker is to use if he or she intends

---

[9] For a summary of Grice's theory of meaning and references to the articles in which he develops it, see Richard Grandy and Richard Warner (eds.), *Philosophical Grounds of Rationality: Intentions, Categories, Ends* (Oxford: Oxford University Press, 1986).

to mean so-and-so by uttering a sentence of such-and-such form. The mood-operators '⊢' and '!' figure prominently in these procedures. For example, using 'U' for utterer and 'H' for hearer (and simplifying slightly from the text (see p. 54)):

(1) U to utter to H ⊢ p if U wills (that) H judges (that) U judges p.

(2) U to utter to H ! p if U wills that H judges that U wills that H wills that p.

Here '⊢ p' represents a sentence in the indicative mood, and '! p' a sentence in the imperative mood. (1) links '⊢' to judging and (2) links '!' to willing. Such links are one reason that, as we noted earlier, Grice thinks "it is legitimate to apply devices, which are initially presented as structural elements underlying mode-differences expressed in *speech*, to the representation of the content of thought, and in particular of the content of *acceptance-in-thought*" (71).

This provides *some* support for his treatment of practical and alethic acceptability by showing that the mood-operators are not unique to that endeavour but play an important theoretical role elsewhere. However, the decisive theoretical consideration would be that we can explain things using the general notion of acceptability that we cannot explain as well without it. Grice does not demonstrate such a theoretical need, nor does he try. We might look in three places for the relevant theoretical need.

The first is Grice's theory of meaning. The theory postulates systematic relations between speech and thought, and it may be that these are best expressed in terms of 'Acc', '⊢', and '!' in ways that take advantage of the occurrence of mood-operators in both the specification of content of thought and the underlying structure of sentences. This may seem confused. We introduced '⊢' and '!' in conjunction with 'Acc', where 'Acc' meant, "it is rationally acceptable that", and this, indeed, is how Grice introduces this notation. However, he also uses the notation to ascribe psychological states. He suggests these equivalences (or near equivalences (see p. 71)):

x accepts (thinks) ⊢ p if (indeed iff, perhaps) x judges p.

x accepts (thinks) ! p if (iff) x wills p.

Here, 'accepts' denotes the same acceptability-in-general referred to by the phrase 'It is rationally acceptable that.' So we might rewrite (1) and (2) above as:

(1) U to utter to H ⊢ p if U accepts ! (that) H accepts ⊢ (that) U accepts ⊢ p.

(2) U to utter to H ! p if U accepts ! (that) H accepts ⊢ (that) U accepts ! p.

Perhaps such a reformulation of the theory might yield some explanatory gain through a more explicit connection of mood-operators with psychological states.

A second area of investigation is the attitude of acceptance itself. Perhaps there are principles that are best formulated in terms of a notion of acceptability-in-general; for example, consistency is an ideal applicable to both thought and action, and perhaps we should see consistency as an ideal relevant to acceptance-in-general.

Thirdly, it is perhaps worth thinking about our attitude towards those ultimate ends in the light of which we direct our lives, those ends that we pursue for their own sake. Imagine I have such an end—say, mastering the game of chess. Having the end involves a cognitive attitude: I think of myself as a chess player, and I think of a well-played game as displaying the beauty of forces in dynamic tension; the game reveals the creativity, courage, and practical judgement of the players in an exercise of intuition and calculation akin to both mathematics and art. I am motivated to master chess because I think of it in this way. Why not regard my attitude towards the end as involving a single state of acceptance-in-general with both a cognitive and a motivational dimension?[10]

We could let this suffice for an introduction to Grice's views about acceptability and the Equivocality Thesis except for one thing—what we have said is not exactly what Grice says. I have departed from his presentation because his treatment of the key points we have covered is flawed. In the next section, I argue that we should see our exposition in this section as a viable interpretation—and correction—of what Grice says.

---

[10] I defend such a view in chapter 1 of Richard Warner, *Freedom, Enjoyment, and Happiness* (Ithaca, NY: Cornell University Press, 1987).

III. *What Grice Actually Says*

The first difference between our discussion and Grice's is that ours
centres around the derivation of a practical necessity. This is not
his explicit focus.[11] His goal (at the end of Chapter 4) is to derive
"If ⊢ A only if ⊢ B, then ! A only if ! B". The point is that an alethic
statement entails a practical one. Grice motivates this approach by
noting that the

existence of such cross-barrier inferribilities would be of interest in
more than one way: (1) It would be of interest in itself, as providing some
interesting general logical facts; (2) anyone who regarded practical
acceptabilities as philosophically problematic, but did not feel the same
way about alethic acceptabilities, might be reassured in so far as he could
think of practical acceptabilities as derivable from alethic acceptabilities;
(3) someone who did not regard either variety of acceptability as *specially*
problematic, might well (and no doubt *should*) regard *both* as in need of
philosophical justification, and it would be a step towards such justification to show that, provided certain alethic acceptabilities are justifiable,
certain practical acceptabilities are also justifiable; (4) the display of such
cross-barrier relations might itself be relevant to the prospects of the
"*Equivocality Thesis*". (90–1)

Against this background, we should emphasize that there is really
little difference in basic goals between our approach and Grice's.
We derived a particular practical necessity, "! we do not torture
this person" (and "Acc ! we do not torture this person"). This same
result follows from Grice's approach. The conclusion of his
derivation is: "If ⊢ A only if ⊢ B, then ! A only if ! B." To derive "!
we do not torture this person", substitute for "⊢ A only if ⊢ B" the
statement "⊢ persons are treated with respect only if ⊢ we do not
torture this person."[12] Then substitute for '! A', '! persons are
treated with respect', and, for '! B', '! we do not torture this person'.

---

[11] Necessity is a major theme in the extensive additions Grice made to the
manuscript. Necessity receives less attention in the basic manuscript itself. The
period in which Grice wrote the additions was one in which he was particularly
concerned with Kant, especially the *Foundations of the Metaphysics of Morals* and
The Critique of Judgement.

[12] We used "⊢ (persons are treated with respect only if we do not torture this
person)", but this is equivalent to "⊢ persons are treated with respect only if ⊢
we do not torture this person".

In explaining Grice's views, it seemed more to the point to derive a particular practical necessity to show how alethic and practical acceptabilities can be seen as variations on a notion of acceptability-in-general, and, indeed, our approach is more consistent with Chapter 3, in which he lays the groundwork for Chapter 4 by showing that arguments about what we ought to believe and arguments about what we ought to do have parallel structures. Moreover, deriving a practical necessity is the only evident way to account for the necessity that attaches to the practical 'ought' and 'must'. Grice actually leaves us without an explicit account of necessity in these cases.

Let us turn to another key similarity—and dissimilarity—between our approach and Grice's. The similarity is that both depend crucially on the premiss that "whoever wills the end wills the indispensable means". Grice begins his derivation with this premiss, which, as we noted earlier, he expresses as: "(1) a *fundamental* psychological law that, *ceteris paribus*, for any creature x (of a sufficiently developed kind), no matter what A and B are, *if* x wills A and judges that if A, A only as a result of B, *then* x wills B" (94), and he argues that (1) entails "(2) x wills (it is x's will) that (for any A, B) if x wills that A and judges that if A, A only as a result of B, then x is to will that B" (95). He then contends that (2) is true only if "(3) x *should* (qua rational) judge that (for any A, B) if it is satisfactory to will that A and also satisfactory to judge that if A, A only as a result of B, then it is satisfactory to will B" (95). (3) follows from (2) because "in so far as x proceeds rationally, x should will as specified in (2) only if x judges that if it is satisfactory to will that A and also satisfactory to judge that if A, A only as a result of B, then it is satisfactory to will that B; otherwise, in willing as specified in (2), he will be willing to run the risk of passing from satisfactory attitudes to unsatisfactory ones" (95).

Note that (3)—with its reference to what one "*should* (qua rational) judge"—introduces a reference to rationality into the derivation. Grice thus represents this rational stricture on our judgement as deriving from our nature as rational, willing beings. We will return to this point. A second—related—issue is: why does Grice use 'should judge' in (3) instead of 'Acc ⊢'? He addresses this issue when he remarks that he will use "a common modal which I have not so far associated with any of the sub-varieties of acceptability, namely, the modal 'should'". He adds, "In a certain sense, this is a slight cheat, since my purpose in doing so is to cover up some of the intricacies of detail which would complicate matters if I were to proceed with direct reference to the modals already invoked . . ." (91).[13] This is very puzzling because, as we saw earlier, he actually does explain 'Acc' in terms of "should" ("[a]n initial version of the idea I want to explore is that we represent the sentences (1) 'John should be recovering his health by now' and (2) 'John should join AA' as having the following structures; *first*, a common 'rationality' operator 'Acc' . . ." (50)). On Grice's approach, "should judge" would either be represented by "Acc" alone (meaning "it is rationally acceptable that") or by 'Acc ⊢' (meaning "It is rationally acceptable that it is the case that"). We will return to this issue as well. For the moment, let us continue with Grice's derivation.

He argues that (3) entails

(4) x *should* (qua rational) judge that (for any A, B) if it is satisfactory that! A and also satisfactory that ⊢ if A, A only as a result of B, then it is satisfactory that ! B.

To see the point, note that in (3) 'judge' and 'will' occur *inside* the conditional. Grice's goal in deriving (4) is to eliminate these occurrences. He achieves his goal by replacing 'satisfactory to will that A' with 'satisfactory that ! A', and 'satisfactory to judge that if A, A only as a result of B' with 'satisfactory ⊢ if A, A only as a result of B'. Note the use of '!' in the representation of the psychological states of judging and willing. As we noted earlier, he embraces these (near) equivalences:

(1) x accepts (thinks) ⊢ p if (indeed iff, perhaps) x judges p.
(2) x accepts (thinks) ! p if (iff) x wills p.

This is what justifies using '⊢' and '!' in the context of judging and willing. Grice explains the step from (3) to (4) by arguing that "the satisfactoriness of attitudes of acceptance resolves itself into satisfactoriness (in the sense distinguished in [Chapter 3] of the *contents* of those attitudes (marked by the appropriate mode-markers)" (95).

---

[13] The sentence continues, 'but as I intend shortly to lay bare some of that detail, perhaps my procedure might be regarded as an expository device, and so as only a *temporary* cheat". It is fair to say that the detail is never laid bare in a way that explains the use of "should".

This appeal to "satisfactoriness" requires explanation. In Chapter 3, he explains "satisfactoriness" as follows:

I would regard reasoning as a faculty for enlarging our acceptances by the application of *forms* of transition, from a set of acceptances to a further acceptance, which are such as to ensure the transmission of *value* from premises to conclusion, should such value attach to the premises. By 'value' I mean some property which is of value (of a certain *kind* of value, no doubt). Truth is one such property, but it may not be the only one; and we have now reached a point at which we can identify another, namely, *practical* value (goodness). So each of these should be thought of as special cases of a more general notion of *satisfactoriness*.   (87–8)

Grice asserts the following equivalences (88):

It is satisfactory to will that A if and only if it is satisfactory that ! A.

It is satisfactory to judge that A if and only if it is satisfactory that ⊢ A.

And,

It is satisfactory that ! A if and only if it is good that ! A.

It is satisfactory that ⊢ A if and only if it is true that ⊢ A.

Since 'it is true that' is clearly redundant in the final equivalence, that equivalence becomes: It is satisfactory that A if and only if ⊢ A.

The problem is that, given these equivalences, (3) does not entail (4) but:

(4a) x *should* (qua rational) judge that (for any A, B) if *it is good that* ! A and ⊢ (if A, A only as a result of B), then *it is good that* ! B.

Grice provides no licence to eliminate the occurrences of 'it is good that'; nor should he. It is false that it is good that ! A if and only if ! A. In his notation, '! A' is an expression of intention ("I shall do A"), and I may, of course, fail to intend to do A when it would be good that I so intend. Indeed, I may, as a result of weakness of the will, fail to intend to do A even when I *believe* that it would be good were I so to intend. This failure to eliminate the occurrences of "it is good that" turns out to be problematic, but let us put this aside for the moment and complete the argument.

Grice notes that 'If p and q, then r' is logically equivalent to 'If q, then (if p, then r)' and hence that (4) entails

(5) x *should* (qua rational) judge that (for any A, B) it is satisfactory that ⊢ if A, A only as a result of B, then if it is satisfactory that ! A, then it is satisfactory that ! B.[14]

He adds, "But if x judges that satisfactoriness is, for any A, B, transmitted in this particular way, then: (6) x *should* (qua rational) judge that (for any A, B) (⊢ if A, A only because B, then if ! A, then ! B)." The 'it is good that' problem arises here: (5) does *not* entail (6) but (6a): x *should* (qua rational) judge that (for any A, B) (⊢ if A, A only because B, then if it is good that ! A, then it is good that ! B). Grice completes his argument by contending that if any rational being should judge that (for any A, B) (⊢ if A, A only because B, then if ! A, then ! B), then

(7) For any A, B, ⊢ if A, A only because B, then if ! A, then ! B.

Of course, (5) does not lead to this conclusion, but only to

(7a) For any A, B, ⊢ if A, A only because B, then if *it is good that* ! A, then *it is good that* ! B.

This may be enough to make Grice's point that an alethic statement entails a practical one, but it does not show us how to derive the necessity of a particular action, and showing the latter is, as we have argued, crucial to his project.

It is instructive to compare Grice's derivation with ours. He starts with "He who wills the end wills the indispensable means," represented as: "a *fundamental* psychological law that, *ceteris paribus*, for any creature x (of a sufficiently developed kind), no matter what A and B are, *if* x wills A and judges that if A, A only as a result of B, *then* x wills B" (94). The occurrence of 'wills' and 'judges' in the antecedent and consequent of the conditional are essential to seeing this as a psychological law—such a law, after all, expresses a lawful connection among mental states (or mental states and

---

[14] Grice's actual formulation involves a semantic assent that self-consciously and deliberately imports a—harmless and eliminable—use/mention confusion into the argument. I have taken the liberty of eliminating this.

actions). From this first premiss, he quickly derives (3): "x *should* (qua rational) judge that (for any A, B) *if* it is satisfactory to will that A and also satisfactory to judge that if A, only as a result of B, *then* it is satisfactory to will that B" (95). Now, his problem is to get rid of the occurrences of 'will' and 'judge' so that he can reach his desired conclusion, in which these terms do not occur. As we have argued, this strategy is less than successful.

We avoided this problem in our derivation by representing "Whoever wills the end wills the indispensable means" as

For any A and B, Acc (If ! A, and ⊢ (A only if B); then ! B).

The result Grice wants—"⊢ A only if ⊢ B, then ! A then ! B"— follows trivially, for it follows immediately that

For any A and B, Acc (If ⊢ A only if ⊢ B, then ! A then ! B),

and from this he allows us to derive

For any A and B, If ⊢ A only if ⊢ B, then ! A then ! B.

This follows from the assumption that, in this context, if any rational being must accept that so-and-so, then so-and-so is true (see the step from (6) to (7) above). However, in taking this approach, we give up something Grice wants. We give up treating the principle as a psychological law and treat it instead as an a priori principle in part definitive of what it is to will. Grice would resist this, but our treatment is certainly a possible approach if his more ambitious approach cannot be made to work.

IV. What is it to Reason?

Now let us turn to another objection to Grice's treatment of practical and alethic necessity, an objection he answers at length. He offers his derivation of a practical necessity as an *explanation* of both actions and attitudes. The objection is that merely exhibiting a derivation does not explain anyone's actual thought or action. We can develop this objection using Grice's own views about the nature of reasons. In Chapter 3, he summarizes the view of reasons he developed in Chapter 2:

I distinguished three types of case (if you like, three ways of using the word) with respect to the word 'reason' ('reasons'), which I called the *explanatory* use (case), the *justificatory* use (case), and the *justificatory– explanatory* use (case), which I shall now rename the '*personal*' use (case). They are interconnected ... if someone thinks that a certain set of considerations is a *justificatory* reason for doing, intending, or believing something, and if he in fact does, intends, or believes that thing because he so thinks, then his *personal* reason for actually doing (intending, believing) that thing is that the aforementioned set of considerations obtain; and to state someone did (intended, believed) something for a specified *personal* reason is a special case of giving an *explanatory* reason for his doing (intending, believing) that thing. (67)

When the chief of police refuses to torture the terrorist, his personal reason for doing so is his conviction that torture is wrong. What is the relation between this reason and the derivation (1)–(6) we gave in Section II (or Grice's derivation in the previous section)? What role does the existence of the derivation play in the explanation of the action? The answer lies in the account of reasoning Grice develops in Chapter 1. We give a brief summary of that account and then turn to the question about the explanatory role of the derivation.

Grice emphasizes that reasoning is a goal-directed activity: we engage in reasoning with (typically at least) the intention of producing reasons *relevant to some end in view*. This intentional activity involves the exercise of the ability to make *reason-preserving* transitions, where the transitions are between sets of thoughts or beliefs (or intentions or whatever). A transition is reason-preserving if and only if necessarily, if one has reasons for the initial set, then one does for the subsequent set as well.[15] The ability to make reason-preserving transitions may, like any ability, be impaired or unimpaired. Good reasoning consists in an *un*impaired exercise of the ability to make reason-preserving transitions; reasoning—good or bad—is an exercise that is not *too* impaired. As Grice explains:

the concept of reasoning may be what I might call 'value-paradigmatic'. ... to explain what reasoning is (and maybe what the term 'reasoning' means), it is necessary in the first instance to specify what *good* reasoning

---

[15] I once proposed this to Grice as his view. He agreed, although, as explained in the text, we differed on how to characterize the ability in question.

is, and then to stipulate that 'reasoning' applies to good reasoning and also to sequences which approximate, to a given degree, to good reasoning; the idea of good reasoning is, in a certain sense, prior to the idea of reasoning. (35)

This presentation of Grice's views on reasoning differs somewhat from Grice's own. He writes:

I would regard reasoning as a faculty for enlarging our acceptances by the application of *forms* of transition, from a set of acceptances to a further acceptance which are such as to ensure the transmission of *value* from premises to conclusion, should such value attach to the premises. By 'value' I mean some property which is of value (of a certain *kind* of value, no doubt). Truth is one such property, but it may not be the only one; and we have now reached a point at which we can identify another, namely, *practical* value (goodness). So each of these should be thought of as special cases of a more general notion of *satisfactoriness*. (87–8)

A "faculty" is a capacity or ability, so here he thinks of reasoning as an ability to apply satisfactoriness-preserving "forms of transition". My "reason-preserving" characterization of the transitions aims at the same sort of generality (reasons for belief, reasons for action, and so on). In explaining reasoning as an ability, he places considerable weight on *forms* of transition. He explains the ability as the ability *to apply certain general patterns of argument*, where the satisfactoriness-preserving character of those forms was explained proof-theoretically. We would, for example, explain the satisfactoriness-preserving character of "If p, and if p, then q; then q" proof-theoretically by demonstrating its derivability in some appropriate system. Grice was very attracted to this idea. As he says:

Many, I suspect, would regard it as rational to suppose that what a logical theory (system) does is to systematize a corpus of antecedently given logical necessities, and (perhaps an even more natural supposition) that moral theory does (or would if there *were* such a theory) systematize antecedent given obligations or incumbencies. But the present proposal would disallow these modes of thinking. If incumbencies are moral necessities, and moral necessities are what is demonstrable in an (acceptable) moral theory or system, the system comes first and cannot be informatively characterized as the system relating to incumbencies or moral necessities. Similarly, a logical theory must be characterizable otherwise than by reference to its concern with logical necessities. This reversal of direction I find appealing, particularly as it would emphasize the central importance of the construction of theories or system; no system, no necessity.   (61)

Grice was well aware of the difficulties here,[16] and, unlike him, I think they are insuperable. I do not think that the satisfactory-preserving character of argument forms can be fully explained as a formal property of those forms. We need to appeal to an independently characterized ability to reason. But, we can put this issue to the side. For our purposes, we simply need the idea of reasoning as an intentional activity involving the exercise of the ability to make reason-preserving transitions.

Our focus is on using the account of reasoning to show how a formal derivation of a practical necessity can reveal an agent's personal reason for action, and, for this purpose, it does not matter how the issue we have raised is resolved. Let us continue, then, with Grice's account of reasoning as an ability. He notes that we sometimes exercise this ability by producing fairly detailed and complete step-by-step arguments from explicitly stated premises to an explicitly stated conclusion. "We have available to us . . . what I might call a 'hard way' of making inferential moves; we in fact employ this laborious, step-by-step procedure at least when we are in difficulties, when the course is not clear, when we have an awkward audience, and so forth" (17). But we do not always do this. "Following the hard way [working out a complete step of reasoning steps] consumes time and energy; these are in limited supply and it would, therefore, be desirable if occasions for employing the hard way were minimized. A substitute for the hard way, the *quick way*, which is made possible by habituation and intention, is available to us . . ." (17). The logician Georg Kreisel[17] illustrates the "quick way". Kreisel once published a six-page proof of a theorem; a "complete"

---

[16] The Gödel Theorem, for example, shows that mathematical necessity cannot be identified with provability in a first-order system. Grice was well aware of this point, and his first line of defence was that his talk of "derivability" should not be identified with first-order provability. Even so, there are serious obstacles here, as Paul Benaceraf, among others, has pointed out.

[17] Kreisel is the logician to whom Grice gives the pseudonym 'Botvinnik' in the text. Botvinnik was the World Chess Champion through the middle part of the twentieth century. Kreisel was a professor in the Philosophy Department at Stanford in 1976 when Grice delivered an earlier draft of *Aspects of Reason* as the Immanuel Kant Lectures. The audience, of course, had no trouble decoding the pseudonym.

proof—provided later by others—takes eighty-four pages.[18] This long proof illustrates the step-by-step "hard way". Kreisel's "quick way" leaps over the vast majority of these steps, but it is still reasoning, still an exercise of the ability to make reason-preserving transitions (see pp. 11–12). The fact that we can extend Kreisel's "quick way" reasoning to a complete eighty-four-page derivation plays an important role in our regarding him as reasoning. It shows us that Kreisel's transitions really are reason-preserving, and, given Kreisel's well-established ability in logic and mathematics, the existence of the derivation is a factor in convincing us that Kreisel made his "quick way" steps *because* he saw they were reason-preserving. If we were unable to produce such a derivation, we would have grounds to doubt that Kreisel reasoned well, or perhaps that he reasoned at all (see Grice's discussion of the hapless Shropshire in Chapter 1 who "reasons" in one quick step from the premiss that chickens run around after their heads are cut off to the conclusion that the human soul is immortal).

The existence of a derivation, then, plays a role in the attribution of reasoning in the "quick way" cases, and, by virtue of this role, the derivation also indirectly plays a role in explaining the existence of personal reasons. Recall Grice's explanation of personal reasons: "if someone thinks that a certain set of considerations is a justificatory reason for doing, intending, or believing something, and if he in fact does, intends, or believes that thing because he so thinks, then his *personal* reason for actually doing (intending, believing) that thing is that the aforementioned set of considerations obtain" (67). Kreisel thinks that the premises he explicitly formulates are a justificatory reason for believing the conclusion; *and*, since he reaches that conclusion by reasoning from these premises—that is, by exercising his ability to make reason-preserving transitions

---

[18] The point is *not* that Kreisel's proof is not deductively valid. Reasoning may be incomplete even when the conclusion *does* follow from the premises. From "Everybody loves my baby, but my baby don't love nobody but me" it follows that I am my baby. However, there is a clear sense in which "Everybody loves my baby, but my baby don't love nobody but me; therefore, I am my baby" is not—at least not for most of us—a complete piece of reasoning. A complete piece of reasoning would at least point out that, assuming a universal domain of quantification for 'everybody', if everybody loves my baby, then, since my baby is included in 'everybody', my baby loves my baby. But since my baby don't love nobody but me, I must be my baby.

—we can see him as believing the conclusion "because he does so think", because he believes the premises are a justificatory reason. Our view of Kreisel as reasoning underlies our view of him as having a personal reason, and, since our view of Kreisel as reasoning rests in part on the existence of the derivation, the derivation plays an indirect role in the attribution of the personal reason.

The examples of torturing the terrorist and staying with a daughter can be viewed similarly. In the terrorist-torture case, for example, the chief of police thinks something like, "Torture violates the respect due persons", and "Torturing this person is inconsistent with the respect due persons" (of course he may not *express* these thoughts this way), and he reasons—with gaps—from these thoughts to the conclusion, "We must not torture this person." In the daughter case, I may reason from premises about the importance of my daughter and my commitment to her to the conclusion that I must stay. Such reasoning certainly can and does occur, but—as many will object—it need not. The chief of police may not reason at all. Imagine that the commitment to "We must not torture" was instilled in him from his earliest years and was reinforced by a variety of forms of social conditioning throughout his life. Confronted with the prospect of torture, he does not engage in any relevant reasoning; rather his reaction is immediate and instinctive. A similar point holds for the daughter example. Imagine I am torn between two visions of my life; for a long time, I cannot decide until the emotional currents turn towards staying, and I commit myself to that course—not as a result of reasoning but simply because that is the direction in which I finally find myself turning. A third case: a child darts out from between two cars into the street directly in front of your speeding car. You do not exercise the ability to make reason-preserving transitions at all. Instead, you instinctively swerve to miss the child. We can still have personal reasons in these cases. In the darting-child case, for example, you certainly think you should avoid hitting the child, and this consideration is a justificatory reason for your swerving the car, and, *were you to reason* from the premiss that you should avoid the child, you would reach the conclusion that you should swerve the car. In this counterfactual way, reasoning connects your thought and action, and reveals it as in accord with reason. Your thought that you should avoid the child can, in this way, form part of your personal reason for doing so.

We should return briefly to our opening remarks about meaning and methodology. We noted that Grice's treatment of meaning as well as his general philosophical methodology rested on the existence of an explanatory link between the explicit arguments that we might, but typically do not, construct, and the attitudes and actions that we could justify through those arguments. The foregoing picture of reasoning reveals the explanatory role Grice assigned to explicit derivations even in those cases in which the relevant agent did not actually construct such a derivation. This is as much the point of the treatment of reasoning as the defence of the Equivocality Thesis.

Before we leave Grice's treatment of reasoning we should briefly raise an issue to which he devotes considerable time and effort. Grice's account of reasoning as an ability raises the question of whether everyone has the same capacity to reason. On the face of it, the answer is obviously *no*, as people clearly vary in their ability to reason. This answer, however, does not fit comfortably with his interest in the possibility that "vitally important philosophical consequences can be reached by derivation from the idea of a rational being". It is natural to think of this project as deriving results from a property—rationality—which all (non-defective) persons have, and which is not variable in degree. If the property varies in degree, then the danger is that the desired philosophical consequences (for example, a duty to respect persons) might hold, not for all persons, but only for those possessing rationality in some relevant degree. In an ingenious and insightful discussion, Grice considers various ways in which we may be said to have the same capacity to reason. My aim is simply to note the connection between this discussion and his overall project.

V. *Happiness and the Rationality of Ultimate Ends*

We have sketched the themes that link Chapters 1–4. Chapter 5, "Some Reflections about Ends and Happiness", remains (the relevant discussion actually begins as the conclusion to Chapter 4; for convenience, I will refer to the entire discussion as 'Chapter 5'). Grice turns to a consideration of happiness as part of his consideration of prudential acceptabilities. As he explains:

Kant thought that there is a special sub-class of Hypothetical Imperative (which he called "counsels of prudence") which were like his class of Technical Imperatives, except in that the end *specified* in a full statement of the imperative is the special end of Happiness (one's happiness). To translate into my terminology, this seems to amount to the thesis that there is a special sub-class of, e.g., singular practical acceptability conditionals which exemplifies the structure "it is acceptable, given that let *a* (an individual) be happy, that let *a* be (do) G" . . . (97)

This passage connects the discussion of happiness to the earlier discussion of practical and epistemic acceptability. Still, the consideration of happiness in Chapter 5 seems disjointed from the previous chapters. Except for the passage quoted above, the consideration of prudential acceptabilities does not employ the notation used in Chapter 4, nor does it explicitly employ any of the conceptual framework of the preceding chapters. So, why does Grice include this material?[19] A sufficient answer, surely, is "for completeness and intrinsic interest". However, the conclusion he reaches at the end of Chapter 5 offers a deeper answer.

He ends his consideration of happiness this way:

To resolve such difficulties, an extra-systemic consideration seems to be required, one which will differentiate ends or systems of ends in respect of value. Here . . . I would like to consider the possibility that the idea of happiness-in-general might be determined by reference to the essential characteristics of a human being (rational animal) . . . (134)

With this conclusion, Grice turns from the role of "underlabourer" to the task of seeing if "important philosophical consequences can be reached by derivation from the idea of a rational being" (2). In doing so, he links *Aspects of Reason* to his other works. To take a brief look at these connections, let us ask how we are to "differentiate ends or systems of ends in respect of value".

Grice defends a notion of absolute, unrelativized value. He takes two approaches here. In *Aspects of Reason*, he takes a "genitorial"

[19] Chapter 5 was not part of the Immanuel Kant Lectures given at Stanford University in 1977. The text of these lectures forms the bulk of Chapters 1–4. "Some Reflections about Ends and Happiness" was delivered as a separate piece at a colloquium at Chapel Hill in 1976. When Grice gave the John Locke Lectures at Oxford in 1979 his first four lectures were the same as his Immanuel Kant Lectures. He used "Some Reflections about Ends and Happiness" as his fifth and final lecture and included it in the manuscript of *Aspects of Reason* as Chapter 5.

approach: "the ends involved in . . . happiness-in-general would, perhaps, be the realization in abundance, in various forms specific to individual men, of those capacities with which a creature-constructor would have to endow creatures in order to make them maximally viable in human living conditions, that is, in the widest manageable range of different environments" (134). The idea is that we imagine ourselves as demi-gods creating creatures according to a rational plan of our own devising. Grice sees this project as yielding substantive philosophical results.[20] His second approach gives pride of place to the concept of freedom. As he says in "Actions and Events", "action (full human action) calls for the presence . . . of *reasons*, and these in turn require that the actions for which they account should be the outcome of 'strong' rational evaluation, which, in the case of ends, will not be restricted to valuation by reference to some ulterior end".[21] He does not distinguish sharply between these two approaches, but the two themes in his work are certainly distinguishable.[22]

Grice uses the notion of absolute value in his account of morality. He thinks (or is inclined to think) that "incumbencies are moral necessities, and moral necessities are what is demonstrable in an (acceptable) moral theory or system" (61). An acceptable moral theory would have to contain precepts referring to absolute values. In *Aspects of Reason* he suggests that it

---

[20] Grice worked very hard on this programme from at least 1970 until his death in 1989. His "Reply to Richards" in Grandy and Warner (eds.), *Philosophical Grounds*, contains a useful summary of the programme.

[21] *Pacific Philosophical Quarterly*, 67 (1986), 34.

[22] When Grice and I worked on the third Carus lecture (which became the third chapter in *The Conception of Value*) our discussion was entirely about freedom, not about creature-construction. It was clear that freedom, not creature-construction, was critical to the derivation of absolute value. A personal note about doing philosophy with Paul: to work on the Carus lecture, I drove up from LA on Friday arriving at noon. We began work, drinking inexpensive white wine as the afternoon wore on; switched to sherry as we broke off to play chess before dinner; had a decent wine from Paul's wine cellar with dinner and went back to work after eating. We worked all day Saturday with copious coffee in the morning (bread fried in bacon grease for breakfast) and kept the same afternoon and evening regime as the previous day. Paul did not sleep at all Saturday night while he kept turning the problems over in his head. After breakfast on Sunday, he dictated, without notes, an almost final draft of the entire lecture.

is not too difficult to envisage a body of precepts about how to behave, relating to a single particular person, who is intended to be both agent and beneficiary with respect to the operation of these precepts; nor is it a great additional effort to suppose these precepts to be derivable from a limited number of parent precepts, still however retaining reference to the particular individual, and generally, with the aid of further factual premisses, a system which constitutes a self-help manual for that individual. It seems by no means out of the question that, if the references to that individual are to be irreducible (not eliminable in favour of references to classes of person to which the individual belongs), then ... the manual is a manual for a particular individual (and for no other individual) just because he has 'legislated' (rightly or wrongly) what his ends are to be. I am inclined to think of some more or less articulated egoistic manuals of this sort as underlying morality. (62–3)

This suffices as a brief glance at Grice's concern with absolute value and morality. The point is simply to indicate that *Aspects of Reason* ties into broader themes found in other works.

VI. Conclusion

The goal of this introduction has been schematic. The aim has been to offer a picture of *Aspects of Reason* as a unified work, and we have left untouched much of the rich detail of the work, a work by one of the cleverest and most ingenious philosophers of the twentieth century.

Aspects of Reason

Proem

I find it difficult to convey to you just how happy I am, and how
honoured I feel, in being invited to give these lectures. I think of
this university and this city, which were my home for thirty-six
years, as my spiritual and intellectual parents; whatever I am was
originally fashioned here; and I find it a moving experience to be,
within these splendid and none too ancient walls, once more
engaged in my old occupation of rendering what is clear obscure.
I am, at the same time, proud of my mid-Atlantic status, and am,
therefore, delighted that the Old World should have called me in,
or rather recalled me, to redress, for once, the balance of my having left her for the New. I am, finally, greatly heartened by my consciousness of the fact that that great English philosopher, under
whose aegis I am now speaking, has in the late afternoon of my
days extended to me his Lectureship as a gracious consolation for
a record threefold denied to me, in my early morning, of his Prize.
I pray that my present offerings may find greater favour in his sight
than did those of long ago.

Oxford
1979

Reason and Reasoning

Introduction

The philosophical clarification of the concept of reason, or perhaps of the family of concepts which shelter under that title, is of
interest to me, and to others, for more than one reason. The nature
of reason is an interesting and important philosophical question
in itself: reason is an important member of the class of ideas with
which, as philosophers, we should be concerned. But, beyond that
foundation of interest, there is the fact that more than one philosopher has held the view that vitally important philosophical consequences can be reached by derivation from the idea of a rational
being. Aristotle, for example, thought that he could reach a characterization of the end for man *via* the following steps: the end
for man is the fulfilment of man's function (*ergon*); the function of
man is the optimal exercise of that capacity which distinguishes
him from other kinds of creature; that capacity is reason or rationality; the optimal exercise of rationality is the contemplation of
the truths of metaphysics; so that is the (primary) end for man.
And Kant considered that among the important dividends which
could be derived from the idea of a rational being was the moral
necessity of adherence to the Categorical Imperative.

Now I do not know whether or not any such grand conclusions
can be derived from the concept of a rational being, though I must
confess that I have a sneaking hope that they can, and a nagging
desire to try to find out. Part of my trouble (which is not only
mine) is the difficulty of discovering the rules of the game, of understanding what sort of procedure is to be counted as a derivation;
another part of my trouble is being hopelessly unclear about the
character of the starting point, about what the concept of a rational
being is to be taken to be. So my primary role here will be that of

the under-labourer, to engage in one or two enquiries which might help towards a clarification of the notion of reason or rationality; though I hope that you will forgive me if, just occasionally, I make a speculative sally in the direction of the foothills of the mountain which Aristotle and Kant thought that they could climb, indeed *had* climbed.

In this chapter, I shall devote myself to the idea that if, as it seems not unreasonable to suppose, reason is, of its nature, the faculty which is manifested in reasoning, then it would be a good idea to investigate what reasoning is. In the next two chapters, I shall pursue a parallel link between reason and reasons, with particular attention to the relation between practical and non-practical reasons.

Reason and Reasoning

No less intuitive than the idea of thinking of reason as the faculty which equips us to recognize and operate with *reasons* is the idea of thinking of it as the faculty which empowers us to engage in *reasoning*. Indeed, if reasoning should be characterizable as the occurrence or production of a chain of inferences, and if such chains consist in (sequentially) arriving at conclusions which are derivable from some initial set of premises, and for the acceptance of which, therefore, these premises are, or are thought to be, reasons, the connection between the two ideas is not accidental.

Let us, then, take as a first approximation to an account of reasoning the following: reasoning consists in the entertainment (and often acceptance) in thought or in speech of a set of initial ideas (propositions), together with a sequence of ideas each of which is derivable by an acceptable principle of inference from its predecessors in the set. Many would be inclined to subscribe to two further remarks about such an account: *first*, that the principles of inference which govern reasoning are non-empirical in character; and, *second*, that it is part of the business (possibly, even the prime business) of logical theorists to distinguish the various modes of inference (non-demonstrative as well as demonstrative) which enter into reasoning, and to systematize the principles of each such mode, thereby both explaining and perhaps (as theorists are wont to do) strengthening assent to (or even, in some instances, undermining assent to) the principles of inference which are intuitively found acceptable at a pre-theoretic stage, and so constitute the initial data for the theorist. I shall now enquire into the adequacy of this preliminary account.

Misreasoning

One correction is plainly called for. Not all actual reasoning is *good* reasoning; some is bad, and some is downright appalling. But our preliminary account seems to leave no space for reasoning to go wrong except through the falsity of one or more of its premisses, or (perhaps) through the perverseness of the world in refusing to conform to the conclusion of an impeccable non-demonstrative inference. Obviously, our steps from premisses to conclusions are by no means always well conducted; indeed, in the golden age before logic became a (minor) branch of mathematics, logicians (or writers on logic) paid some attention to fallacies (an interest which could do with revival). We should not, then, commit ourselves to the idea that steps in actual reasoning *are* validly made, but only to the idea that they are thought by the reasoner to be validly made, or (perhaps) to the idea that they are *either* validly made *or* are thought to be validly made. A little further clarification, however, is needed, and there are one or two morals to be drawn. Jack says to Jill (whom he does not yet know very well), "Career women always smoke heavily. You smoke heavily, so you must be a career woman." Does Jill reply, "You evidently accept the principle of inference: 'A's are always B, this is a B: therefore this is an A'; that is not an acceptable principle"? If she made this reply, one would suspect irony. Jack has perhaps argued *as if* he accepted such a principle, but I should resist the supposition that he actually *did* accept it, even temporarily or momentarily. People who reason badly may sometimes accept bad principles of inference; but normally what they do is better thought of as, in some way or other, misapplying good principles. But in what way? Suppose Jill had replied, "You have evidently mistakenly supposed your inference to be of the valid form 'A's are always B's, this is an A; so this is a B'; whereas its actual form was rather 'A's are always B's, this is a B; so this is an A'." Would *this* reply be an improvement on the one previously suggested for her? Not much, I think. People may indeed sometimes mistakenly suppose that their actual reasonings exemplify a *particular* valid principle when, in fact, they do not, and may in consequence reason badly; but I do not believe that this is the normal case, especially with reasonings as simple as the one under examination. Perhaps a better reply for Jill might be: "You seem to be confused, no doubt because that crack on, or in, your crown is still bothering you. I do not accuse you of thinking that the particular invalid form exhibited by your actual argument is a valid form, nor of thinking, wrongly, that your argument was in *Barbara*. I suggest, rather, that the difference between your argument form and *Barbara* did *not* on this occasion present itself to you, and that the similarity between your form and *Barbara* accounts for (as it were, causally) your supposition that the individual argument which you produced was a valid argument."

The principal points which seem to me to be, so far, emerging are three in number. (1) Generally, though not invariably, bad argument does not have its own bad principles of inference, but rather arises from a misapplication of valid principles. (2) That our reasonings should exhibit valid principles is not merely something which usually obtains, nor merely something which both usually obtains and is believed by the reasoner to obtain, but is something which we, as reasoners, *want* to obtain. (It may even be something which *should* obtain, and something which we try to realize, but these contentions have not yet been argued.) (3) A belief or a desire that a particular piece of reasoning does or should conform to valid principles does not entail (though it does not exclude) a belief or a desire that it does or should conform to a *particular* valid principle. The operation of individual principles may be, and perhaps for a specifiable class of cases *should* be, quasi-causal. The meaning of "quasi-causal" of course awaits explication.

I hope that, as we go on, some or all of these points will be expanded and corroborated. Before embarking on the next sub-topic, however, I should like to suggest for consideration a hypothesis of a somewhat more general character. The discrimination and systematization of acceptable principles of inference provide for us a model, or rather, perhaps, an infinite set of models, by reference to which we may understand actual reasonings (an ideal construction to which actual reasonings approximate). Such models or ideal constructions are models in three ways: (1) they are *analytic* models, since it is an adequate degree of approximation to them which confers on certain sequences of thought the title of Reasoning; (2) they are *explanatory* models, in that they provide (or play a central part in providing) accounts of how actual reasoning proceeds, and why it so proceeds; (3) they are *normative* models, in that they provide patterns of the ways in which actual reasoning *should* (ought to) proceed. If one were in a fanciful mood, one might be tempted to say that inferential validity is at once the formal cause, the efficient cause, and the final cause of reasoning. My suspicion is that not only do these models possess this triple aspect, but it is no accident that they do; that there is a conceptual province for which these three aspects go together, and that this conceptual province is specially connected with living creatures. Unless I am quite mistaken, a detailed and systematic development of this conjecture would be profoundly valuable.

'Incomplete' Reasoning

A further batch of questions arises in connection with what I shall call 'incomplete' reasoning, or 'not fully explicit' reasoning (though these labels may be mildly question-begging). Subject to correction from a maturer reflection, we may have on our hands two kinds of case: (*a*) that in which the incomplete reasoning may be converted into reasoning which conforms to canonical standards of respectability by the addition of further premises which the reasoner has in mind, either (i) explicitly or (ii) subliminally; and (*b*) that in which there are no such further premises which the reasoner has in mind, but the reasoner thinks that such premises exist even though he does not know what they are. It may turn out that further refinement of this dichotomy is required. The rough distinction just drawn embodies two possible answers to the main problem raised by incomplete reasoning, namely, how canonical inference patterns are to be deployed to meet the obvious fact that most actual reasonings do not overtly conform to them, but are (for example) enthymematic.

Let us begin with a very simple example of the kind of argument which it is traditional to classify as an enthymeme. When

Jack sustains his head injury, Jill, putting Jack's concerns before her own, says (or thinks), "He is (you are) an Englishman, so he (you) will be brave." There seem to be three ways of treating this example. (1) In line with the tradition of syllogistic logic, we might suppose that Jill's reasoning involves, as a "suppressed premiss", the proposition that Englishmen are always brave, and that Jill has this proposition in mind, perhaps explicitly (if she is talking) or subliminally (if she is thinking). Her *full* argument, which includes the suppressed premiss, is canonically valid; but only a truncated version of her actual reasoning is expressed (in speech or in thought). There are, of course, difficulties connected with the idea of subliminal thinking; but these are very *general* difficulties and so perhaps should not be pressed in this particular case. Aside from them, there is a special difficulty; someone who knows what Jill has said or thought might be inclined to comment, "That does not follow;" and he would be disposed towards this comment *not* because of the banal fact that the expression of Jill's argument is not canonical in form, but because he regards it as being false that Englishmen are always brave. But on the present treatment this comment would be inappropriate, since the proposition in question is *a premiss* of her argument (her full argument), and the falsity of a premiss plainly does not entail that an inferentially licensed conclusion does not *follow* from its premisses. (2) We might regard "Englishmen are always brave" as expressing not a *premiss* of Jill's argument but (perhaps in a slightly misleading way) the specific principle or rule of inference of that argument. To be a little more precise, we can suppose that we have, for 'informal' argument, what might be called inference-schemata; expressed with a ruthless contempt for use and mention which will be characteristic of these lectures, one of them will run: "To infer from Fa to Ga if whatever satisfies 'F' also satisfies 'G' "; on the (contingent) assumption that whatever satisfies 'Englishman' also satisfies 'brave', we can derive the specific rule "To infer from *a is an Englishman* to *a is (will be) brave.*" This option, if adopted, would allow (for informal argument) contingent (or contingently based) inference rules, though not necessarily contingently based inference-schemata. (3) Possibly the most attractive idea is to suppose that we should consider ourselves faced not just with *one* argument or piece of reasoning (Jill's actual reasoning), but with *two*, one of which is actual (Jill's reasoning) and the other of which is non-actual or ideal (a reconstruction of Jill's argument incorporating as a premiss the proposition which we are taking her to have had non-explicitly in mind): the former will be informal, the latter formal (and often canonical). Jill's actual argument will be (informally) valid just in case there is a legitimate reconstruction of it which is formally valid and which supplements the informal argument with premisses which are true (as well as being propositions which, in some sense, Jill has in mind). This suggestion preserves the idea that the 'unexpressed' proposition is a suppressed *premiss*, and also the idea that inferential rules are non-contingent (since no special rules other than those of formal inference are invoked for informal inference); this suggestion would, I think, always be operable if the previous suggestion were operable (and vice versa). I shall proceed as if I accepted this third option.

Another possible source of trouble is now visible. We have so far been assuming that the suppressed premiss in Jill's argument is "Englishmen are always brave". But why should we make this assumption? The suppressed premiss could be "Englishmen are brave", "Englishmen are normally brave", "Englishmen are usually brave", "Englishmen are likely to be brave", and maybe there are further possibilities. Some or all of these other candidates, if chosen, would make the reconstructed argument non-demonstrative in character, but apart from a possibly false premiss and false conclusion it could remain a respectable member of its kind (whatever that kind might be). These thoughts prompt the reflection that, in the contretemps envisaged in my previous section, Jack might have a killing answer to Jill's last reply; he might say, "*You* are evidently assuming that my argument from the premisses *Career women always smoke heavily* and *you smoke heavily* to the conclusion *you are a career woman* was a *deductive* argument. If your logical education had been a little less narrow, it would have occurred to you that, taken as a *non-deductive* argument, there is nothing wrong with it." But how is one to resolve the kind of indeterminacy which is now appearing, and making difficult the selection of a reconstructed argument? By asking the arguer? By invoking a Principle of Charity, to attribute to the arguer that reconstruction which is logically most satisfactory, or least unsatisfactory? If we choose the latter, what is the foundation of such a principle?

Troubles of this kind become even more acute when we move to the consideration of less trivial examples; to examples, that is, in which the gap between explicit premises and conclusion is, intuitively, far greater. Let me offer an extreme specimen. When I was an Oxford undergraduate, there was a contemporary of mine whose name I cannot remember; it was the name of some English county, so let us call him 'Shropshire'. His career at Oxford did not last very long; an unsurprising fact—given that, at an early philosophy tutorial, he claimed that the immortality of the soul is proved by the fact that, if you cut off a chicken's head, the chicken will run round the yard for a quarter of an hour before dropping. Was that an instance of reasoning? Before you answer, let me produce another real life story for comparison with the one I have just given: about twenty years ago a distinguished logician, whose identity I will conceal under the name 'Botvinnik', published a proof, or the sketch of a proof, of an (alleged) theorem; his 'proof' was six pages long. Two Harvard graduate students (one now himself a distinguished logician) set themselves to expand Botvinnik's proof. They found the conclusion of it to be indeed a theorem; but their expansion was eighty-four pages in length.

Now, I have an 'expansion' of Shropshire's 'argument'. It runs as follows:

If the soul is not dependent on the body, it is immortal.

If the soul is dependent on the body, it is dependent on that part of the body in which it is located.

If the soul is located in the body, it is located in the head.

If the chicken's soul were located in its head, the chicken's soul would be destroyed if the head were rendered inoperative by removal from the body.

The chicken runs round the yard after head-removal.

It could do this only if animated, and controlled by its soul.

So the chicken's soul is not located in, and not dependent on, the chicken's head.

So the chicken's soul is not dependent on the chicken's body.

So the chicken's soul is immortal.

If the chicken's soul is immortal, *a fortiori* the human soul is immortal.

So the soul is immortal.

The question I now ask myself is this: why is it that I should be quite prepared to believe that the Harvard students ascribed their expansion of Botvinnik's proof, or at least some part of it, to Botvinnik (as what he had in mind), whereas I have no inclination at all to ascribe any part of *my* expansion to Shropshire? Considerations which at once strike me as being likely to be relevant are:

(1) that Botvinnik's proof without doubt contained more steps than Shropshire's claim;

(2) that the expansion of Botvinnik's proof probably imported, as extra premisses, only propositions which are true, and indeed certain; whereas my expansion imports premisses which are false or dubious;

(3) that Botvinnik was highly intelligent and an accomplished logician; whereas Shropshire was neither very intelligent nor very accomplished as a philosopher.

No doubt these considerations are relevant, though one wonders whether one would be much readier to accord Shropshire's production the title of 'reasoning' if it had contained some *further* striking 'deductions', such as that since the soul is immortal moral principles have absolute validity; and one might also ask whether the effect of (3) does not nullify that of (2), since, if Shropshire was stupid, why should not one ascribe to him a reconstructed argument containing plainly unacceptable premisses? But, mainly, I would like some further light on the following question: if such considerations as those which I have just mentioned are relevant, why are they relevant?

I should say a word about avowals. The following contention might be advanced. If you want to know whether someone R, who has produced what may be an incomplete piece of reasoning, has a particular completion in mind, the direct way to find out is to ask him. That would settle the matter. If, however, you are unable to ask him, then indirect methods will have to be used, which may well be indecisive. Indeterminacy springs merely from having to rely on indirect methods. I have two comments to make. First: it is far from clear to what extent avowals do settle the matter. Anyone who has taught philosophy is familiar with the situation in which, under pressure to expand an argument they have advanced, students, particularly beginners, make statements which, one is inclined to say, misrepresent their position. This phenomenon is perhaps accounted for by my much more important second point: that avowals in this kind of context generally do not have the character which one might without reflection suppose them to have; they are not so much *reportive* as *constructive*. If I ask someone if he thinks that so-and-so is a consequence of such-and-such, what I shall receive will be primarily a *defence* of this supposition, not a report on what, historically, he had in mind in making it. We are in general much more interested in whether an inferential step is a good one to make than we are in what a particular person had in mind at the actual moment at which he made the step. One might perhaps see an analogy between avowals in this area and the specification of plans. If someone has propounded a plan for achieving a certain objective, and I ask him what he proposes to do in such-and-such a contingency, I expect him to do the best he can to specify for me a way of meeting that contingency, rather than to give a historically correct account of what thoughts he had been entertaining. This feature of what I might call inferential avowals is one for which we shall have to account.

Let us take stock. The thesis which we proposed for examination has needed emendation twice, once in the face of the possibility of bad reasoning, and once to allow for informal and incomplete reasoning. The reformulation needed to accommodate the latter is proving difficult to reach. Let us take s and s′ to be sequences consisting of a set of premises and a conclusion (or, perhaps it would be better to say, a set of propositions and a further proposition), or a sequence (sorites) of such sequences. (This is not fully accurate, but will serve.) Let us suppose that x has produced s (in speech or in thought). Let "formally cogent" mean "having true premises, and being such that steps from premises to conclusions are formally valid".

(1) We cannot define "s is a piece of reasoning by x" as "x thinks s to be formally cogent", because if s is an incomplete piece of reasoning s is *not*, and could not reasonably be thought by x to be, formally cogent.

(2) We cannot define "s is a piece of reasoning by x" as "(∃s′) (s′ is an expansion of s and s′ is formally cogent)" because (*a*) it does not get in the idea that x thinks s′ formally cogent and (*b*) it would exclude bad reasoning.

(3) We cannot define "s is a piece of reasoning by x" as "x *thinks* that (∃s′) (s′ is an expansion of s and s′ is formally cogent)", for this is too weak, and would allow as reasoning any case in which x believed (for whatever reason, or lack of reason) that an informal sequence had some formally cogent expansion or other. (Compare perhaps Shropshire.)

(4) We cannot define "s is a piece of reasoning by x" as "(∃s′) (s′ is an expansion of s and x thinks s′ to be formally cogent)" because of the indeterminacy which bedevils the search for such expansions; there may not be a definitely identifiable expansion which meets this condition.

So what are we to suggest on behalf of the provisional thesis?

Too Good to be Reasoning

I have so far been considering difficulties which may arise from the attempt to find, for all cases of actual reasoning, reconstructions of sequences of utterances or explicit thoughts which the reasoner might plausibly be supposed to think of as conforming to some set of canonical patterns of inference. I turn now to a different class of examples, with regard to which the problem is not that it is difficult to know how to connect them with canonical patterns, but rather that it is only too easy to make the connection. Like some children (not many), they are too well behaved for their own good.

Suppose someone says to me, "John has arrived," and I reply, "I conclude from that that John has arrived." Or he says, "John has arrived and Mary has also arrived," and I reply, "I conclude that Mary has arrived." Or he says, "My wife is at home," and I reply, "I reason from that that someone is at home." Is there not something very strange about the presence in my replies of the verbs "conclude" and "reason"? It is true, of course, that if instead of my first reply I had said, "So John has arrived, has he?" the strangeness would have been removed; but here the word "so" serves not to indicate that an inference is being made, but rather as part of an idiomatic way of expressing surprise (one might have said, "Well, fancy that!"). Now having spent a sizeable part of my working life exploiting it, I am not unaware of the distinction between a statement's being false, and its being true but misleading or in-appropriate or pointless, and on that account a statement which it would be improper, in one way or another, to make. But I don't find myself lured by the idea of using that distinction here.

Suppose, again, that I were to break off the chapter at this point, and switch suddenly to this argument: "I have two hands (here is one hand and here is another). If had three more hands, I would have five. If I were to have double that number I would have ten, and if four of them were removed six would remain. So I would have four more hands than I have now." Is one happy to describe this performance as *reasoning*? There is, however, little doubt that I have produced a canonically acceptable chain of statements.

Or suppose that, instead of writing in my customary free and easy style, I had framed my remarks (or at least the argumentat-ive portions of my remarks) as a verbal realization, so to speak, of sequences of steps in strict conformity with the rules of a nat-ural deduction system of first order predicate logic; I give, that is to say, an updated analogue of a medieval disputation. Would those brave souls who continued to read be likely to think of my per-formance as the production of reasoning, or would they rather think of it as a crazy formalization of reasoning conducted at some pre-vious time?

The points suggested by this stream of rhetorical questions may be summarized as follows:

(1) Whether the samples presented fail to achieve the title of "reasoning", or whether they achieve it by the skin of their teeth, perhaps does not very greatly matter; for whichever way it is, they seem to offend against something (different things in different cases, perhaps) very central to our conception of reasoning.

(2) *Mechanical* applications of ground rules of inference, either singly or in concatenation, are reluctantly (if at all) called reasoning. Such applications may perhaps legitimately enter into (form indi-vidual steps in) authentic reasonings, but they are not themselves reasonings, nor is a string of them.

(3) There is a demand that a reasoner should be, to a greater or lesser degree, the author of his reasonings. Parroted sequences are not reasonings when *parroted*, though the very same sequences might be reasoning if not parroted.

(4) Some examples are deficient because they are aimless or pointless. Reasoning is characteristically addressed to *problems*: small problems, large problems, problems within problems, clear problems, hazy problems, practical problems, intellectual problems; but *problems*.

(5) A *mere* flow of ideas minimally qualifies as reasoning, even if it happens to be logically respectable. But if it is directed, or even monitored (with intervention should it go astray, not only into fallacy or mistake, but also into such things as irrelevance), that is another matter.

(6) Finicky over-elaboration of intervening steps is frowned upon, and in extreme cases runs the risk of forfeiting the title of reasoning. In speech such over-elaboration would offend against conversational maxims, against (presumably) some suitably formulated maxim of Quantity. In thought, it will be branded as pedantry or neurotic caution. At first sight, perhaps, one would have been inclined to say that greater rather than lesser explicitness is a merit; not that inexplicitness is *bad*, but that, other things being equal, the more explicitness the better. But now it looks as if proper explicitness is an Aristotelian mean, and it would be good some time to enquire what determines where that mean lies.

The burden of the foregoing observations seems to me to be that the provisional account of reasoning, which has been before us, leaves out something which is crucially important. What it leaves out is the conception of reasoning as an *activity*, as something with goals and purposes; it leaves out, in short, the connection of reasoning with the *will*. Moreover, once we avail ourselves of the great family of additional ideas which the importation of this conception would give us, we shall be able to deal with the quandary which I laid before you a few minutes ago. For we could say (for example) that x reasons (informally) from A to B just in case x thinks that A and *intends* that, in thinking B, he should be thinking something which would be the conclusion of a formally valid argument the premisses of which are a supplementation of A. This will differ from merely thinking that there exists some formally valid supplementation of a transition from A to B, which I felt inclined not to count as reasoning.

I have some hopes that this appeal to the purposiveness of authentic reasoning might be sufficient to dispose of the quandary on which I have directed it; but I am by no means entirely confident that this is the case, and so I offer a second possible method of handling the quandary, one to which I shall return in a later chapter when I shall attempt to place it in a larger context.[1] We have available to us (let us suppose) what I might call a 'hard way' of making inferential moves; we in fact employ this laborious, step-by-step procedure at least when we are in difficulties, when the course is not clear, when we have an awkward audience, and so forth. Inferential judgements, however, are normally desirable undertakings for us only because of their actual or hoped for destinations, and are therefore not desirable for their own sake (a respect in which, possibly, they may differ from inferential *capacities*). Following the hard way consumes time and energy; these are in limited supply and it would, therefore, be desirable if occasions for employing the hard way were minimized. A substitute for the hard way, the *quick way*, which is made possible by habituation and intention, is available to us, and the capacity for it (which is sometimes called intelligence, and is known to be variable in degree[2]) is a desirable quality. The possibility of making a *good* inferential step (there being one to be made), together with such items as a particular inferer's reputation for inferential ability, may determine whether on a particular occasion we suppose a particular transition to be inferential (and so to be a case of reasoning) or not. On this account, it is not essential that there should be a single supplementation of an informal reasoning which is supposed to be what is overtly in the inferer's mind, though quite often there may be *special* reasons for supposing this to be the case. So

[1 See also 'Reply to Richards', in Richard Grandy and Richard Warner (eds.), *Philosophical Grounds of Rationality: Intentions, Categories, Ends* (Oxford: Oxford University Press, 1986), and *The Conception of Value*, ed. Judy Baker (Oxford: Oxford University Press, 1991).]

Editor's notes are enclosed in brackets to distinguish them from Grice's own notes.

[2 See the discussion of 'flat' and variable rationality in the next section, where Grice discusses variation in degree. Grice interpolated this paragraph here in 1988. The surrounding text was complete in 1987.]

Botvinnik is properly credited with a case of reasoning, while Shropshire is not.

What Can't Logic Catch?

I have, so far, been mainly (though not exclusively) considering problems connected with the task of relating the actual reasonings of ordinary people to patterns of complete argument some of which will be valid by canonical standards, and a systematization of which will be (hopefully) provided by formal logic. It is now time to ask whether there may not be some essential features of reasoning which logic cannot capture, not because logic is not yet sufficiently fully developed (because we need more logical systems), but because those features are not of the right *sort* to be represented in a logical system at all.

Consider the following example: an unfortunate professor has undertaken, many months previously, to give ten formal lectures to a certain institution, and one month before the starting date the institution asks him for the titles of the individual lectures. He reasons as follows: "Oh, God: It's all a mess; I have piles of material, but none of it seems worth listening to, and it isn't in shape, and I am in a terrible muddle. And if I give them the ten titles I had in mind I'm not sure that they will fit what (if anything) finally emerges. It's always like this; I take something on long in advance, and then when the time comes I'm reduced to pulp. Why do I do it? Why don't I learn? I'd like to cancel the whole thing. However, I said I would do it, and if I cancel my name will be mud, so I must go through with it somehow. Anyway, I'm probably not in a fit state to make a proper judgement about the value of my material. I can see they must have titles, and I can't think of anything better than the ones I had in mind, so I'll give them those and ask for latitude to depart from them if need be. And I'll get four lectures done by the starting date, and that will give me some leeway once they begin."

Such monologues as these are commonplaces in our lives; and not only monologues, since much reasoning is couched in dialogue. Now I spoke of the poor professor as reasoning, and some might question the description (I am none too confident myself). But I find my reluctance to accept it dwindling when it occurs to me that, while my monologue certainly contained sentences which could not happily be prefixed by the phrase "he reasoned that . . .", it may well be that items which are not cases of *reasoning that* are elements in, and crucial elements in, specimens of *reasoning*; much as pausing to tie one's shoelace, or to look at the view, is not itself *strictly* an instance of walking, but may nevertheless be a very relevant element in something which *is* an instance of walking, namely, a walk. Should the description be allowed, then many actual reasonings contain such things as questions, the raising of real or imagined objections, suggestions of hypotheses, and even expressions of feeling. Are we confident that, in so far as such items are relevant to the character of reasoning, the logic of the future will be able, or even should try, to devise representation of them? Or that, if the logician should not try, there is not a region which someone *else* should investigate systematically? For some of these features of actual reasoning will be extremely relevant to personal attributes which we take to be characteristic of good reasoners, like the ability to construct interesting hypotheses, to keep to the point, to point to analogies, to know when *not* to ratiocinate, and so on. And even if a formal depiction of these features were accessible, it is not clear that it would be sufficient as a basis for the attribution of the corresponding qualities; in natural deduction systems there are devices which mark that an assumption is being made, so we can imagine a device which represents hypothesization; but detection of this mark might leave us in the dark about whether the represented hypothesization was a *good* one to make. And to represent order is not to represent orderliness. We are perhaps encountering a question which is an analogue to a notorious problem in ethics, to reach a satisfactory account of the relative priority (one way or the other, or in different aspects both ways) of goodness in a man and the goodness of his acts. Indeed, the kind of features which I am attending to may belong to a department of ethics; that, indeed, was where Aristotle seemed to locate them (or something not *too* different from them), when he devoted part of *Nicomachean Ethics* VI to a discussion of intellectual excellences. But to relegate them to a kind of ethics would not itself solve problems; and perhaps I might conclude with a brief sketch of the way I feel inclined to regard the issues I am now raising.

The picture which I would like to suggest starts with the idea that, when we explore the nature of rationality, or ask what it is to have reason, we really have at least two concepts on our hands, which we should get our hands on. One is a 'flat', non-degree-bearing, non-variable concept; it is this concept which applies when it is said that man is a rational being. In respect of this concept no man is *more* or *less* rational than any other. The other is a variable, degree-bearing concept, and here some men are definitely more rational than others (though perhaps some philosophers would not agree: Descartes *may* have thought that not only was God not so niggardly as to leave it to Aristotle to make men rational, but he was not so unjust as to make one man more rational than another). The second concept is intimately connected with the first; and, further, differences in respect of the second concept are differences in *value*: it is better to be more rather than less rational. Concepts linked in this kind of way are not uncommon; a man may know how to drive a car in the sense that he knows how to operate the controls in such a way as to get the car along the road, but he may know how to drive a car in the further and related sense that he *sure* knows how to drive a car, that he is a *good* driver. Now, if reasoning is thought of as the exercise of reason, and 'reason' (or 'having reason') is open to both a flat and a variable interpretation, we have at once a possible explanation of some of the phenomena which have emerged during this chapter. Hesitation, for example, over the application of the expression 'reasoning' to the aimless or trivial specimens which I produced for you might be accounted for by the fact that such specimens might be called 'reasoning' if reasoning is thought of as a manifestation of 'flat' reason, but not so called if reasoning is thought of as a manifestation of 'variable' reason; and specimens which enter into reasoning but are not instances of *reasoning that* might be specimens which are relevant to assessments in respect of variable reason without being instances of flat reason.

It might help to expand the characterization of these two concepts of rationality if I invoke a somewhat hackneyed item in philosophers' analogies, namely, chess, and consider a partial analogy between rationality and chess-capacity. Flat chess-capacity will consist in knowing and being able to apply the laws of chess (including, of course, the moves), much as flat rationality consists in a capacity to apply rules of inference. Variable chess-capacity, expertise at chess, will be learned not from the rule-book, but by practice combined with, perhaps, instruction from other players and such works as *Modern Chess Openings* and Fine on the endgame. It essentially consists in being good at activities (chess games) conducted in accordance with the laws of chess, much as variable rationality consists in being (more, or less) good at activities conducted in accordance with the laws of reasoning, that is to say, at reasonings of one sort or another. For activities of a certain sort to be something one can be (more or less) *good at*, they must be directed towards goals; these goals may vary, from occasion to occasion, and they may be more or less specific and more or less ultimate; in chess we find such goals as victory, and also more local and intermediate goals, like strengthening one's position by establishing a knight on KB5; in reasoning we have as goals the solution of problems, which may be less specific and more ultimate, like understanding Kant's first version of the Categorical Imperative, or more specific and less ultimate, like understanding what a maxim is supposed to be (as a step towards the solution of the former problem). Both in chess-playing and in the exercise of rationality we find rough distinctions, in particular cases, between strategies and tactics; and the content of these, and the direction of the sequence of moves which they govern, will be dependent on the identity of the goals which are being pursued.

Not only will (what I might call) *policies* which are manifested in particular chess games and particular reasonings be more or less specific, and stand in relations of subordination to one another, but also *excellences* in the two domains may be subordinated to one another. Just as excellence at chess may be diversified, in that one player may be better at openings and less good at the endgame than another, or it may be that nobody handles a pair of bishops like Fischer, so does variable rationality preside (so to speak) over subordinate excellences. But now we must begin to take account of obvious differences between our analogues. Chess-playing is not *about* anything, whereas reasoning is always reasoning *about* some topic or question, which may fall within some special area like mathematics or theology; so not only are there specific rational excellences or qualities with respect to mathematics, which some may have in a greater degree than others, but one may be good at mathematical reasoning while quite incompetent at theological reasoning. However, we seem to be willing to allow the attribution of general excellence, or quality, of reasoning as well as that of specialized quality; and general excellence seems also to be diversified. This licence we allow ourselves may be a consequence of the fact that general rational excellences (or some of them) seem to be special cases of capacities for achieving qualities which are desiderata for any practical undertaking, qualities like simplicity, economy, accuracy, inventiveness, and so on. Another derivative of the fact that reasoning is *about* things is that reasoning may be directed upon itself; one may not only use reasoning to plan a hen-house or a cathedral, but, if the first-level task is sufficiently formidable, one may plan how to plan a cathedral; one may even plan a philosophical methodology, though too few people do. A consequence of the last two observations, that general rational excellence is diversified and that reasoning may be turned on itself (together, perhaps, with some further premiss), is that we may be able to treat flat reason, not merely as something which is necessarily manifested in manifestations of variable reason, but as providing an inferential base for determining the nature of variable reason itself and, also, of its more specific subordinate competences (excellences). We might be able to argue, for instance, along the following lines.

(*a*) Let us assume that it can be shown that truth (or, better, some more general feature which will include truth as a special case, but will also apply to some of the objects of psychological attitudes other than belief, such as desire) is a *value* (in the sense of *desideratum*).

(*b*) Inferential rules, which flat rationality is the capacity to apply, are not arbitrary, in that they pick out transitions of acceptance in which transmission of satisfactoriness (including where appropriate truth) is guaranteed or (in non-deductive cases) to be expected.

(*c*) Since our actually making such transitions in a particular case is up to us (and subject to our particular needs and circumstances), inferential rules can be seen as directives (the precise kind of which remains to be determined) observance, or non-violation, of which is a desideratum.

(*d*) Since reasoning is (and it may be of its essence that it is) sometimes addressed to problems, at least sometimes reasoning has a particular goal, which the reasoner aims at reaching. Reasonings then are at least sometimes characterizable as successful or not successful.

(*e*) Some particular qualities, exhibited in reasonings, can be characterized as certain or likely to lead to success (or, perhaps, failure) in pursuit of goals in reasoning, irrespective of the particular nature of those goals.

(*f*) In so far as no sources of information (no premisses) other than the nature of the flat capacity of reason (and implicata thereof) have been used to reach such a characterization, at least *some* excellences are determinable as such by "the concept of a rational being".

Now, if such arguments are possible, their conclusions may not be of the grand sort which rationalists have hoped to draw from the idea of a rational being, but at least they would be substantive conclusions; and they might be of value towards the grander enterprises, both as providing possibly usable premisses and because the derivation of them would help to clarify the methodology of those enterprises.

A Final Point

These reflections might be reinforced by an approach from another quarter, namely, a consideration of the ordinary use of the words 'rational' and 'reasonable' (and their complementaries). One might have expected that, when used as terms of praise, these words refer to very general qualities of reason (in which case one would be right), and indeed to the *same* quality (in which case one would be wrong). A few examples. It might be unreasonable of me to expect my wife to clean my football boots for me, but it would not be irrational. I may well have bought those boots at a very reasonable price, but it is not very clear how I might have bought them at a very rational price. To cheat someone in a business deal (as such) is neither unreasonable nor irrational; it is merely somewhat repulsive; to cheat a man when you knew you might be found out, and as a result lose a valuable client, I would regard as a better candidate for 'unreasonable' than for 'irrational'; to cheat him when you knew it was quite likely that you would be found out, and when, if you were, you would lose your job at a time when employment was very difficult to obtain, I would call 'irrational'. Yielding to a tempting invitation to go out drinking when I have already decided to spend the evening working on tomorrow's lecture, I would regard as (as such) neither unreasonable nor irrational, though it may be weak, and foolish. To yield to that temptation when I have not yet decided what to do, but know I really ought to get on with that work for tomorrow, *might* be unreasonable but would not be irrational. If I have bunglingly got my firm into a difficulty, and I go and confess the matter to my boss, he might be both reasonable about it and rational about it; he might be reasonable about it in that he was not too hard on me, and rational about it in that he coolly and in a reasoned way told me what was the best course to take.

Now I cannot give you a detailed solution to the problem of distinguishing between "rational" and "reasonable", not only because I do not have the time, but also because I am by no means sure what to say. But I do think that I know two keys to the solution of this problem. The first key is that "reasonable", unlike "rational", is really a *privative* term; "unreasonable" is, as some were once wont to say, the "trouser-word" in this particular pair of complementaries. To be reasonable is to be (relatively) free from unreasonableness; and to be *very* reasonable is to be free from a high degree of unreasonableness which one might (or some might) have been expected to exemplify or display in the circumstances. The second key is provided by Aristotle; in *Nicomachean Ethics* I, he remarks that both the ratiocinative and the non-ratiocinative (or desiderative) parts of the soul may have reason; the former *intrinsically*, as the source of rational principles or precepts, the latter *extrinsically*, as heeding or listening to those principles or precepts. My idea is to link the first of Aristotle's interpretations of "having reason" with the word 'rational', and the second with the word 'reasonable'. In application to behaviour, to be rational is to possess (or, on a given occasion, to display) the capacity to reach principles or precepts relating to conduct; to be reasonable is (in general or on a particular occasion) to be free from interference, on the part of desire or impulse, in one's following such principles or precepts.

The present relevance of this discussion is that ordinary thought and speech embody the idea of reason as *regulation*, as something which should control desire or passion. So the phenomenon of incontinence should not be regarded, as it too often has been, as a stumbling block to some otherwise attractive theory of will and practical reason; if reason is regulation, then it must be possible for what is regulated to get out of hand, and this possibility should be provided for, in the theory, from the start. Furthermore, if we incorporate, in our idea of reason, the idea of it as regulation of a sub-rational nature which may get out of hand, we have enlarged the "concept of a rational being" from which philosophically significant conclusions might be derivable, and so given such derivations a better chance of success. It is curious that both Aristotle and Kant, despite their sophistication with regard to the nature of practical reason, should have slipped up here in their different ways, that both should have succumbed to the fascination of the purely intellectual being. Both of them, it seems to me, at crucial moments thought of the rationality, the realization of which must be the supreme end for a rational being, as being the *distinctive element* in such a being, considered in isolation from other elements necessarily present in, but not necessarily peculiar to, such a being; so for Aristotle the primary end for man becomes approximation to the activity of a pure substance, and for Kant the practical law is something which has to be applicable to a being with a *holy will*, treated not just as a possibly useful fantasy, but as a being which might actually exist. This common ingredient in their practical philosophies seems to me to have been restrictive rather than beneficial.

Reason and Reasons

Introduction

Though the main topic of this chapter and the next is Reasons, together with some more detailed questions pertaining thereto, it might be a good idea for me, before embarking on that matter, to give a brief résumé of the principal suggestions which I made in the previous chapter, particularly as I should like to add one or two reflections before leaving the subject of Reasoning. I took, as a stalking horse, a thesis which characterized reasoning as (roughly) the production in thought, or speech, of a sequence of ideas (propositions) consisting of an initial set (ultimate premisses) together with further members each of which is derivable, by canonical (formally valid) principles of inference, from its predecessors in the sequence. In comment on this thesis I proceeded on five main lines.

(1) That emendation was plainly required in view of the fact that not all reasoning is *good* reasoning, even though, normally, even bad reasoning uses, or misuses, *good* principles of inference. The obvious emendation would be to substitute for "derivable by canonical principles" the phrase "thought by the reasoner to be derivable by canonical principles".

(2) That further trouble arose from the obvious fact that most actual reasoning is informal, or 'incomplete' (for example, enthymematic), and therefore such that no sane reasoner could suppose his reasonings, as they stand, to conform to canonical principles of inference. The natural emendation, namely, that the sequence, which is to be supposed to conform, or to be thought by the reasoner to conform, to canonical principles, is not the actually produced sequence but an expansion of it, incorporating

additional premisses which the reasoner supposedly has in mind, itself ran into difficulties; for either the so-amended thesis merely demands that the reasoner should think that there exists such an expansion (without, perhaps, having any idea what it is), in which case some examples (for example, the "Shropshire" example) would undeservingly receive the title of reasoning; *or* the amended thesis demands that the reasoner have a particular supplementation in mind, in which case the indeterminacy which in many actual cases afflicts attempts to identify such a supplementation, would disqualify from being reasonings examples which one would wish to allow *as* reasonings.

(3) That a consideration of sequences which are "too good to be reasonings" (too well-behaved) prompted the thought that the provisional thesis had left out a central characteristic of reasoning, namely, its connection with the *will*; more particularly, that reasoning is typically an *activity*, with goals and purposes, notably the solution of *problems*. Once this feature is recognized, there seems to be an easy solution to the quandary set up in (2); for we may think of the reasoner as *intending* his production of the conclusion *to be* the production of something which is an informal consequence of his premiss (premisses), a state of affairs which is evidently distinguishable from merely thinking that a certain proposition is, somehow or other, informally derivable from a given set of propositions.

(4) That attention to a further class of reasonings (like the poor professor's lament) suggested that there is a not at all clearly demarcated range of features which reasonings possess, and which are by no means irrelevant to their character as reasonings, but which it would be vain to ask logicians to try to capture. The status of such features might be to some extent illuminated if we distinguish between reason as a flat (non-variable) capacity (the capacity to apply inferential rules) and reason as a variable (degree-bearing) capacity, in which interpretation it is an excellence or competence, and is differentiated into a variety of subordinate excellences or competencies. Further, the two interpretations may well not be disconnected; for it might be possible to derive from the notion of reason as a flat capacity, together with the information that it is to be deployed in the solution of problems, an a priori identification of some or all of the special competencies into which

'variable' reason is differentiated; and such a derivation might be regarded as a modest success in a programme of deriving (practical consequences) from the concept of a rational being.

(5) That the concept of a rational being would be enlarged, and its potentialities as a derivational source enhanced, if it is allowed as an essential feature of reason that it is to be regulative of a pre-rational self containing such elements as appetites and feelings.

Flat and Variable Rationality

It is now time I think to pursue a little further, with a beadier eye and a less rhetorical style, the examination of the suggested distinction, and the sketched connection, between 'flat' and 'variable' reason (rationality). According to the picture presented which I would call Picture (1), there is a kind of rationality (R^1) which is

(1*a*)　non-variable (flat, not admissible of differences of degree);

(1*b*)　basic (ultimate with respect to—not definable in terms of—variable rationality);

(1*c*)　non-valuational (the attribution of R^1 is not an ascription of merit or demerit);

(1*d*)　central to (essential to) the type (and maybe also to the tokens of the type) *Rational Being* [alternatively, central to being a *non-deformed*, non-maimed, Rational Being];

(1*e*)　underlying one or more kinds of rationality (R^2, R^3, . . .), which are

(2*a*)　variable;

(2*b*)　valuational (in that differences of degree with respect to R^2 (R^3, . . .) are or involve differences in value).

And to say that R^1 underlies R^2 is to mean that the status of R^2 as a dimension of or excellence (and of some or all specifications of R^2 as subordinate dimensions of excellence) is derivable, by some appropriate method of derivation, from (*a*) the (inescapable) fact that subjects of such excellence (rational beings) possess R^1, together perhaps with (*b*) certain further facts of high generality.

Opposed to Picture (1), one might envisage an upholder of Picture (2), the central idea of which would be that, while it may well be

possible to identify a flat concept of rationality as well as a variable concept, any flat concept there may be will not be basic, but
will in fact arise from a variable concept of rationality by the impos-
ition thereon of one or another form of limitation; and that being
so, since the flat concept will be *positioned* in the variable concept,
the former concept cannot provide a foundation for the valuational
status of the latter.

There is a variety of considerations which might be involved in
an attempt to support Picture (2), or to assail Picture (1). One part
of such a campaign might be to comment adversely upon the highly
schematic character of Picture (1), as presented, and to demand
an increase in definition which might not be easy to find. Picture
(1) seems to leave undetermined even crucial items: we are not given
a characterization of the class of qualities which are specifications
of variable rationality; we are not told what modes of derivation
are to be used to establish these qualities as dimensions of excellence; we are not provided with a clear identification either of flat
rationality or of whatever auxiliary premisses will be needed for
such accusations. Until these gaps are filled (it may be said) there
is no thesis to discuss.

These animadversions might be accompanied by some further
salvoes. It might be argued that Picture (2) rather than Picture (1)
accords with the standard situation with respect to related flat and
variable attributes; in such cases it is generally the case that the
flat concept arises by some kind of limitation imposed on the variable concept; a large house (flat-largeness) is one which is larger
(has a higher degree of variable largeness—or size) than most houses,
and so for most examples. There is (it might be said) a reason to
suppose this conceptual pattern to apply to the particular case of
flat and variable rationality. There is more than one candidate for
the title (on some interpretation or other) of flat rationality; for
example, it might be possible to be rational in the sense of being
'adequately rational' or 'perfectly rational', that is, of *not* suffering
from any of some favoured class of failings or deficiencies; this primitive sense of 'rational' could be used to pick out a certain level of
positive rationality (variable), such as a *respectable* level thereof.
But any such concepts as these, though flat and non-basic, would
have no claim to be universal (or near-universal) features of human
beings. The most relevant, therefore, of possible flat concepts would

be one which could be represented as applicable to any creature with *some degree or other* of (variable) rationality, whose measure of rationality is not zero. In so far as such a model of flat rationality can be rigorously applied, it will entail that no determinate level of rationality above zero is the largest possible level (above zero); so Picture (2) will escape the embarrassment of having to claim (as Picture (1) claims) that there is a specifiable minimal competence which characterizes all rational beings, a claim which, to the extent that Picture (1) as the core of their rationality relies on the analogy with chess, seems to involve attributing to all rational creatures, as the core of their rationality, an unfailing competence with respect to certain rudimentary inferential moves. Such an attribution (it may be suggested) is nothing but a latter-day revival of the Cartesian idea [*Regulae*] of the infallibility of deduction, and is no more acceptable now than it was then.

An accurate assessment of the merits of the contenders in the kind of confrontation which I have just staged is rendered doubly difficult by two lacunae in recent philosophical enquiry; there is, so far as I know, no adequately systematic treatment of the logical characteristics and implications of the family of concepts which includes such items as capacities, capabilities, aptitudes, powers, potentialities, and other related ideas; nor is there available a thoroughgoing study of the relations between variable and non-variable attributes. But despite this handicap, some sort of reply can, I think, be made to the advocate of Picture (2). One might begin by suggesting that to regard Picture (1) (as presented) as being a *thesis*, even a vague thesis to be *first* sharpened and *then* examined for truth, may not be the best way of looking at it. As is not unusual with philosophical ideas, it may be illegitimate to demand or expect that Picture (1) be *first* clarified and *then* tested for truth; there may be no viable method of *separating*, even in thought, exposition from criticism, in which case the cry "You first tell me what you are maintaining, and then we can see whether it is correct" may be quite out of place. Picture (1) is better regarded as a research project than as a hazily expressed thesis;[1] and the most realistic way of implementing it might be somewhat as follows. Without having as yet any very clear idea of the proper way to

---

[1] I am at this point indebted to discussion with Dan Isaacson.

characterize or determine the boundaries of variable rationality, we obtain, from intuition or from the standard assumptions made by philosophers or other theorists, some set of qualities which appear to be intellectual excellences, and also to be of a kind which, intuitively, *ought* to be established as excellences by the method sketched in Picture (1), if *any* excellences are so attributable. This list might consist in, for instance, such items as clear-headedness, a sense of relevance, flexibility, and inventiveness.[2] Making a provisional assumption that such items are establishable, one then enquires what kind of method of derivation, and what minimum range of initial premises relating to the essential character of rational beings (treated, perhaps, at this point as identifiable with *human* beings) and their condition or environment would be sufficient to confer upon the items in question their assumed status as excellences. If this undertaking yields results then one enquires what *other* admissible excellences are derivable from this material, and what general characterization one could give of the range of derivable excellences, being prepared to make adjustments to any list of excellences, my characterization thereof, any group of premises, and any system of derivation, should such adjustment yield a better theoretical structure (by whatever standards the merits of such structures are judged). If these efforts are persistently unrewarded, or are little rewarded, one abandons the enterprise, and with it Picture (1).

This predominantly Aristotelian methodology might perhaps be enriched by a more Kantian underpinning. It might be possible to produce an argument, in advance of a clarification, sharpening, and construction justification of Picture (1), to the effect that some structure or other of the kind schematically described in the initial presentation of that picture is rationally demanded; it might

---

[2] *Candidates for specialized R-excellences* (application (*a*) to people; (*b*) to logical operations, states, etc.)

Clear-headedness	Breadth
Thoroughness	Sense of relevance
Tenacity in argument	Intellectual caution
Flexibility	'Nose' (intuitiveness)
Orderliness	Inventiveness
	Subtlety
	Memory

be contended that, in advance of knowing about the appropriate list of excellences which fall under the heading of variable rationality, what method of derivation is to be employed, and what precisely the premisses of such a derivation are to be, there is a good reason to accept the idea that there must be a non-variable concept of rationality (whatever its composition may be) from which whatever excellences there may be, which are determinations of variable rationality, derive somehow or other their status. Now I cannot myself, as of now, propound such an argument (though I suspect that there may be one); but I think I can point to a poor relation of such an argument, namely, a general argument which would at least cast doubt on Picture (2), even if it did not directly support Picture (1). In a fashion which certainly owes a debt to Aristotle's distinction between *dunameis alogoi* and *dunameis meta logou*, one might distinguish a variety of types of capacity. First we might point to a sub-class of capacities the fulfilments of which are not admissible objects of endeavour: whether because to talk that way would be nonsensical or because the cash value of what one was saying would be totally obscure, we would not be ready to allow that someone could be seeking or trying to actualize on a particular occasion the human capacities of growth or of digestion, though of course one might perfectly well seek to foster those capacities (perhaps by taking pills). Other capacities are such that one can seek their fulfilment at a particular moment; I can for example make up my mind to knit a pair of socks this afternoon. But the presence of the endeavour is by no means necessary either for knitting or for exercising (realizing) one's capacity to knit. If wearing my night-cap, with my eyes closed, and snoring like a bursting dam, I sit clacking away with knitting needles and a sweater steadily takes shape, it seems to me that I may be both knitting and exercising my capacity to knit. Furthermore, if I am a total nitwit at knitting, I might in a waking state be trying to knit but not knitting. Sometimes, however, trying to x (to do something which in fact is instantiated in x) is a *necessary* condition for x-ing, or for realizing a capacity for x-ing, or for both. It seems to me plausible to suppose that for one to compose a limerick about the Absolute, or for me to exercise, with respect to the Absolute, my capacity for composing limericks, it is required that I should be seeking (trying, meaning) to compose a limerick, or at least to do something of a sort such that intentionally to do something of that sort is to compose a limerick. Sometimes, again, it seems that trying to x is *sufficient* for x-ing; if I am trying to treat you with respect, it may be that (at least on one reading of the phrase) I *am* treating you with respect, and am perhaps also exercising (in one sense) my capacity for treating people with respect, no matter how ham-handedly I in fact behave.

Now it seems that, if we could maintain (to speak, for a moment, a little loosely) that in the case of the capacity which constitutes rationality (variable rationality), the exercise of this capacity even in the lowest degree has, both as a necessary condition and as a sufficient condition, that the exercise is *seeking* to exercise rationality, then we would have given an argument which would undermine Picture (2), in so far as Picture (2) implies that there is no minimal degree of positive, variable rationality. For if *seeking* to be rational (to exercise rationality) is tantamount to being rational, then one is not being more or less rational in accordance with the degree to which one's performance is successful in meeting certain standards of performance. To put the matter a little more accurately, suppose that we start with certain material conditions for rational performance $P_1, \ldots P_n$, which we will call conditions for proto-rationality. These might include such things as following certain primitive inferential rules. Further suppose that for X to perform/behave rationally is for X to produce some performance and with the intention that, in performing, he should be fulfilling the conditions for proto-rationality, or some particular one (or more) of these conditions; and, that for X to be rational is for X to have the capacity to perform rationally. Inadequacy in conforming to the conditions for proto-rationality will not lower his degree of rationality, since that depends, not on the facts of his performance, but on the purpose behind it. Loss of rationality as a capacity can be achieved only if X is, or becomes, incapable of *seeking* or trying to be rational (to exhibit rationality). The prospects for this argument depend, of course, on the possibility of supporting the initial supposition, namely, that rationality is a capacity for the actualization of which, on an occasion, it is *both* necessary *and* sufficient that its actualization on that occasion is aimed at or sought for; though I shall not attempt here to support that claim, I am inclined to think that it could be supported.[3]

It is worth noting that the course of this discussion has begun to exhibit a striking analogy with a certain once-fashionable problem in ethics, the relation between (as they used to say) doing one's duty and acting from a certain motive, in particular a sense of duty. *Just as* exercising rationality might be represented as consisting in doing something from the thought that to do that thing is to conform to dictates of reason, *so* acting dutifully (doing one's duty) consists in doing something from the thought that to do that thing is to conform to the dictates of duty. It might be worth getting this problem down from its dusty shelf; for if the analogy is established it may not be long before some alert philosopher, remembering Kant, seeks to explain the analogy by hypothesizing that the capacity for morality is a special case of rationality.

Now, while it might be that the argument, which I have been sketching, makes it difficult to uphold Picture (2), it is by no means clear that the supporter of Picture (1) has been given much cause for rejoicing; for the argument might also be unfavourable to the idea of a basic flat rationality which serves as a foundation for excellences in respect of variable rationality. Indeed it may be important to see that these are not the only pictures in the gallery. I shall now suggest a third picture, applying it in the first case to the concept of reasoning, with the idea that a parallel pattern might be applied to rationality.

There are three observations I should like to make. All involve, I think, the adumbration of further questions which very much deserve exploration, exploration which, in the case of some or all of them, would generate enquiries likely to be large in both scope and depth.

---

[3] Pattern A (Picture (2))

(a) X exhibits rationality^F *iff* x exhibits *some* degree of [variable] rationality^V.
(b) No minimum (determinate) degree of rationality^V.

Pattern B (Picture (1))

(a) X exhibits rationality^F *iff* x seeks to exhibit proto-rationality.
(b) There may be degrees of proto-rationality, but to be rational^F x does not have to exhibit any of these; he might fall off the scale of proto-rationality, but fall within (non-variable rationality) since he is seeking to fall on scale or proto-rationality. [One who has no proto-rationality may still be rational^F, since rationality^F is a matter of seeking proto-rationality.]

(1) The thought that bad reasoning normally, though perhaps not invariably, uses, or misuses, the same inferential principles as good reasoning ('good' principles) prompts in me the further thought that the concept of reasoning may be what I might call 'value-paradigmatic'. Its position may not be like that of such concepts as those of (say) a climate, a mountain, or a shower of rain (though even here I have some questions), where it can be independently specified what is to count as an instance of the concept, and *then*, should there be a need, standards of valuation can subsequently be invoked and specified, so that distinction can be made between climates which are good and those which are not. It is rather that to explain what reasoning is (and maybe what the term 'reasoning' means), it is necessary in the first instance to specify what *good* reasoning is, and then to stipulate that 'reasoning' applies to good reasoning and also to sequences which approximate, to a given degree, to good reasoning; the idea of good reasoning is, in a certain sense, prior to the idea of reasoning. It is, to my mind, a crucially important question what is the *range* of value-paradigmatic concepts; how far do they extend? It does not require very sharp eyes, but only the willingness to use the eyes one has, to see that our speech and thought are permeated with the notion of purpose; to say what a certain kind of thing is is only too frequently partly to say what it is for. This feature applies to our talk and thought of, for example, ships, shoes, sealing wax, and kings; and, possibly and perhaps most excitingly, it extends even to cabbages. I suspect that it applies to items which are related, in one or another of a variety of ways, to the notion of *life* (including that notion itself). It seems, moreover, a short step from allowing that a certain piece or segment of thought or vocabulary is impregnated with the notion of *purpose* to allowing that it is impregnated with the notion of *value*. Now the possibility that one might have to accord a wide range to value-paradigmatic concepts could hardly be bad news to the 'far-out' rationalist, who wants to derive significant substantial conclusions from the idea of a rational being; and it might very well be bad news to the far-out descriptivist, who wishes to interpret or reconstruct our language so as to free it from valuational mythology. To eschew value-notions in scientific enquiry is one thing (which may well be laudable); to make the same ideal part of one's philosophical methodology is

quite another thing; totally to lop off valuation might carry with it a total lopping off of usable description.

(2) I have tried to make use of the notion of intention to distinguish between (*a*) reasoning from A to B (thinking that A, and so that B) and (*b*) thinking that B is a consequence of A, and thinking that A and thinking that B. This suggests to me that inferential rules have two aspects or, if you like, two versions; a *descriptive* version (for example, 'B is a consequence of A', or 'A implies B') and a *prescriptive* version (for example, *either* 'if you accept A, then accept B' *or* 'if you accept A, then you *ought* to accept B'). These aspects or versions will of course be systematically related. But it is not at all clear how the prescriptive version should be formulated; for example, the first of the patterns I have just mentioned ('if you accept A, then accept B') will hardly prove satisfactory. If I were conscientious about observing rules of inference, and were familiar with the inferential rules needed to prove geometrical theorems, and *then* were unfortunate enough to look at Euclid's axioms, I should be chained to my desk until Judgment Day, dutifully deriving theorems from axioms, theorems from theorems, and so on. I would be the first to allow that Euclid's work was good, but hardly *that* good. How, then, should prescriptive versions be formulated in a less demanding way?

(3) I have talked undiscriminatingly about subsidiary excellences (competences) falling under the generic notion of excellence of reason. But there are plainly some distinctions to be made; we should at least need a distinction between excellences which are *specificatory* of excellence at reasoning, and those which are *ancillary* to such excellence. Just as good eyesight is indispensable for excellence at tennis, but (unlike having a powerful service) is not itself a part of excellence at tennis, so having a reasonably good memory (unlike critical acumen) is not *itself* an excellence of reason. How are such distinctions as this to be more fully characterized?

To return from methodological sermonizing, if the idea of value-paradigmatic concepts has merit, then it may be no more difficult to suppose that rationality (or reason) is such a concept than to suppose that reasoning is. This supposition with respect to rationality will give us Picture (3). I pass on now to a consideration of the general nature of reasons.

Reasons

I think we may find, in our talk about reasons, three main kinds of case.

(1) The first is that class of cases exemplified by the use of such a sentence as "The reason why the bridge collapsed was that the girders were made of cellophane". Variant forms would be exemplified in "The (one) reason for the collapse of the bridge was that ..." and "The fact that the girders were made of cellophane was the (one) reason for the collapse of the bridge (why the bridge collapsed)", and so on. This type of case includes cases in which that for which the (*a*) reason is being given is an *action*. We can legitimately use such a sentence form as "The reason why he resigned his office (for his resigning his office) was that p"; and, so far as I can see, the same range of variant forms will be available. I shall take as canonical (paradigmatic) for this type of case (type (1)) the form "The (a) reason why A was (is) that B".

The significant features of a type (1) case seem to me to include the following.

(*a*) The canonical form is 'factive' both with respect to A and to B. If I use it, I imply both that it is true that A and that it is true that B.

(*b*) If *the* reason why A was that B, then B is the *explanation* of its being the case that A; and if *one* reason why A was (that) B, then B is *one* explanation of its being the case that A, and if there are other explanations (as it is implicated that there are, or may be) then A is overdetermined; and (finally) if *a part* of the reason why A was that B, then B is a part of the explanation of A's being so. This feature is not unconnected with the previous one; if B is the explanation of A, then both B and A must be facts; and if one fact is a reason for another fact, then it looks as if the connection between them must be that the first explains the second.

(*c*) In some, but not all, cases in which the reason why A was that B, we can speak of B as causing, or being the cause of, A (A's being the case). If the reason why the bridge collapsed was that the girders were made of cellophane, then we can say that the girders' being made of cellophane caused the bridge to collapse (or, at least, caused it to collapse when the bus drove onto it). But not in all cases; it might be true that the reason why X took offence was that all Tibetans are specially sensitive to comments on their appearance, though it is very dubious whether it would be proper to describe the fact, or circumstance, that all Tibetans have this particular sensitivity as the cause of, or as causing, X to take offence. However, it may well be true that if B does cause A, then the (or a) reason why A is that B.

(*d*) The canonical form employs 'reason' as a count-noun; it allows us to speak (for example) of *the* reason why A, of there being *more than one* reason why A, and so on. But for type (1) cases we have, at best, restricted licence to use variants in which 'reason' is used as a mass-noun. "There was considerable reason why the bridge collapsed (for the bridge collapsing)" and "The weakness of the girders was some reason why the bridge collapsed" are oddities; so is "There was good reason why the bridge collapsed", though "There was *a* good reason why the bridge collapsed" is better; but "There was (a) *bad* reason why the bridge collapsed" is terrible. The discomforts engendered by attempts to treat 'reason' as a mass-noun persist even when A specifies an action; "There was considerable reason why he resigned his office" is unhappy, though one would not object to, for example, "There was considerable reason *for* him to resign his office", which is *not* a type (1) case.

(*e*) Relativization to a person is, I think, excluded, unless (say) the relativizing 'for X' means "in X's opinion", as in "for me, the reason why the bridge collapsed was . . .". Again, this feature persists even when A specifies an action: "For him, the reason why he resigned was . . ." and "The reason for him why he resigned was . . ." are both unnatural (for different reasons).

I shall call type (1) cases "reasons why" or "explanatory reasons".

(2) The cases which I am allocating to type (2) are a slightly less tidy family than those of type (1). Examples are:

"The fact that they were a day late was some

(a) reason for thinking that the bridge had collapsed."

"The fact that they were a day late was a reason for postponing the conference."

We should particularly notice the following variants and allied examples (among others):

That they were a day late was reason to think that the bridge had collapsed.

There was no reason why the bridge should have collapsed.

The fact that they were so late was a (gave) good reason for us to think that . . .

He had reason to think that . . . (to postpone . . .) but he seemed unaware of the fact.

The fact that they were so late was a reason for wanting (for us to want) to postpone the meeting.

I shall take as the paradigmatic form for type (2) "That B was (a) reason (for X) to A", where "A" may conceal a psychological verb like "think", "want", or "decide", or may specify an action.

Salient features seem to me to include the following.

(*a*) Unlike type (1), where there is double factivity, the paradigmatic form is non-factive with respect to A, but factive with respect to B; with regard to B, however, modifications are available which will cancel factivity; for example, "If it were (is) the case that B, that would be a reason to A."

(*b*) In consonance with the preceding feature, it is not claimed that B explains A (since A may not be the case), nor even that if A *were* the case B *would* explain it (since someone who actually does the action or thinks the thought specified by A may not do so because of B). It is, however, in my view (though some might question my view) claimed that B is a *justification* (final or provisional) for doing, wanting, or thinking whatever is specified in A. The fact that B goes at least some way towards making it the case that an appropriate person or persons should (or should have) fulfil (fulfilled) A.

(*c*) The word "cause" is still appropriate, but in a different grammatical construction from that used for type (1). In Example (1), the fact that they were so late is not claimed to cause anyone to think that the bridge had collapsed, but it is claimed to be (or to give) cause *to* think just that.

(*d*) Within type (2), 'reason' may be treated *either* as a count-noun *or* as a mass-noun. Indeed, the kinds of case which form type (2) seem to be the natural habitat of 'reason' as a mass-noun. A short version of an explanation of this fact (to which I was helped by George Myro) seems to me to be that (i) there are no degrees of explanation: there may be more than one explanation, and something may be a part (but only a part) of the explanation, but a set of facts either does explain something or it does not. There are, however, degrees of justification (justifiability); one action or belief may be more justifiable, in a given situation, than another (there may be a better case for it). (ii) Justifiability is not just a matter of the *number* of supporting considerations, but rather of their *combined weight* (together with their *outweighing* the considerations which favour a rival action or belief). So a mass-term is needed, together with specifications of degree or magnitude.

(*e*) That B may plainly be a reason for a person or people to A; indeed, when no person is mentioned or implicitly referred to, it is very tempting to suppose that it is being claimed that the fact that B would be a reason for anyone, or any normal person, to A.

One might call type (2) cases "justificatory reasons" or "reasons for (to)".

(3) Examples:

John's reason for thinking Samantha to be a witch was that he had suddenly turned into a frog.

John's reason for wanting Samantha to be thrown into the pond was that (he thought that) she was a witch.

John's reason for denouncing Samantha was that she kept turning him into a frog.

John's reason for denouncing Samantha was to protect himself against recurrent metamorphosis.

If X's reason for doing (thinking) A was that B, it follows that X A-ed because B (because X knew (thought) that B). If X's reason for doing (wanting, etc.) A was to B, it follows that X A-ed in order to (so as to) B. The sentence form "X had several reasons for A-ing, such as that (to) B" falls, in my scheme, under type (3), unlike the seemingly similar sentence "X had reason to A, since B", which I locate under type (2).

The paradigmatic form I take as being "X's reason(s) for A-ing was that B (to B)".

Salient features of type (3) cases should be fairly obvious.

(*a*) In type (3) cases reasons may be either of the form *that B* or of the form *to B*. If they are of the former sort, then the paradigmatic form is doubly factive, factive with respect both to A and to B. It is always factive with respect to A (A-ing). When it is factive with respect to B, factivity may be cancelled by inserting "X thought that" before B.

(*b*) Type (3) reasons are "*in effect explanatory*". If X's reason for A-ing was that (to) B, X's *thinking* that B (or *wanting* to B) explains his A-ing. The connection between type (3) reasons being, in effect, explanatory, and their factivity is no doubt parallel to the connection which obtains for type (1) reasons. I reserve the question of the applicability of "cause" to a special concluding comment.

(*c*) So far as I can see, "reason" cannot, in type (3) cases, be treated as a mass-noun. This may be accounted for by the explanatory character of reasons of this type. We can, however, here talk of reasons as being *bad*; X's reasons for A-ing may be weak or appalling. In type (2) cases, we speak of there being *little* reason, or even *no* reason, to A. But in type (3) cases, since X's reasons are explanatory of his actions or thoughts, they have to *exist*. (I doubt if this is the full story, but it will have to do for the moment.)

(*d*) Of their very nature, type (3) reasons are relative to persons.

Because of their hybrid nature (they seem, as will in a moment, I hope, emerge, in a way to partake of the character both of type (1) and of type (2)) one might call them "Justificatory–Explanatory" reasons.

I am now in a position to formulate a systematizing hypothesis concerning the interrelations of the three types of case. (i) Type (3) reasons are, in effect, special cases of Type (1) reasons; they explain, but *what* they explain are actions and certain psychological attitudes. (ii) They are also closely connected with Type (2) reasons; if X's reason for A-ing is that B, it is *not* necessarily the case that the fact that B *does* justify X's A-ing; but it *is* necessarily the case that X *regarded* (even if only momentarily or subliminally) the fact that B as justifying him in A-ing. The presence to X of a certain consideration B as *his* (type (3)) reason for A-ing requires the presence, in X, of a belief that B is a *type (2)* reason for him to A. (iii) Though actions and certain psychological attitudes are

Type	Canonical form	Features (i) Factivity, (ii) Explanatoriness, (iii) Cause, (iv) Mass- or Count-Noun, (v) Person-relativization
(1) Pure Explanatory	That B is (was) a (the) reason why A (The reason why A was that B)	(a) Factive (A); Factive (B) (b) B explains A (c) For non-general B, B causes A to be the case (that A) (d) 'Reason' count-noun, never mass-noun (e) Person-relativization excluded
(2) Justificatory	That B is (was) (a) reason (for X) to A	(a) Non-factive (A); Factive (B) (b) B need not explain A, but justifies A (c) B is (a) cause (for X) to A (not A to be the case (that A)) (d) 'Reason' count-noun *and* mass-noun (e) Person-relativization not excluded
(3) Hybrid (Justificatory–Explanatory)	X's reason(s) for A-ing was (were) that B (to B)	(a) Factive (A): Factive for 'that B', non-factive for 'to B' (b) Thought (desire) that B explains A (c) X's thought that (to) B *not* cause of X's A-ing, nor (invariably) cause for X to A (d) Reason count-noun, never mass-noun (e) Person-relativization demanded

FIG. 1. Classification of reasons

sometimes explained by type (3) reasons, this is not invariably the case. Something which explains X's action or X's attitude *may* be something not correctly described as X's reason for doing that action or adopting that attitude. It might be that the reason *why* X embraced the policeman was that he was very drunk, or that the reason *why* X prodded the doorman's stomach was that it looked to him like a balloon. What *made* X do something, or *impelled* him to do it, will often be a type (1) reason for doing it without being a type (3) reason. Such items are not type (3) reasons because they are not thought of by X as justificatory. Fig. 1 summarizes these relations among the various types of reasons.

Two footnotes to conclude this section.

(1) Consider the following example: "The fact that a dandelion derives its energy from photosynthesis is a reason for it to have leaves." (*a*) This example resembles type (2) examples, since, if the cited fact really *is* a reason for a plant to have leaves, it will at the same time be something which *justifies* the plant's having leaves. But (*b*), unlike standard type (2) examples, in this case what is a reason for X's doing or being such-and-such is *not ipso facto* a reason for X's *wanting* to do or be such-and-such, nor for someone other than X to want X to be such-and-such; for dandelions do not have wants, and it is doubtful if any human being wants a dandelion to have leaves. Further, (*c*), some have taken reasons of this sort to provide a certain kind of *explanation* of X's being such-and-such (for example, of a dandelion's having leaves). If this be so, then we have justificatory reasons which explain the existence of the states of affairs which they justify, and do this without the mediation of a type (3) reason.

Difficulties of this sort lead some theorists to deny the existence of reasons of this special sort, to reject at least *this* kind of 'final cause'. I am unhappy with such a course; in company with Aristotle and Kant, and other illustrious persons, I am inclined to think that final causes play an indispensable role in the foundations of ethics.

(2) The fact that if B is a (type (2)) reason to A, B can also be said to be (give) cause to A, shows that in one not negligible sense type (2) reasons are causes. Those, however, who debate whether reasons are causes usually (I think) have in mind type (3) reasons.

If we consider the vernacular use of "cause", it is fairly plain that type (3) reasons are *not* causes, at least of that for which they are reasons. My love of cricket, which (let us say) was my reason for playing yesterday, may have caused me to neglect my work, but did not (in the vernacular sense of 'cause') cause me to play yesterday. But, of course, the debate is not really about whether reasons are causes in the vernacular sense; it is about whether to specify a type (3) reason as the explanation of an action is to give a "causal explanation" of the action, in a sense of "causal explanation" which is none too clear to me, and which (I sometimes suspect) is none too clear to the disputants.

I can now show my hand a little with regard to the future chapters. In the next two chapters I shall go into some detailed questions about justificatory reasons, with particular concern about the relation between the practical and the non-practical varieties of this kind of reason. After that, I hope to pay some attention to the matter of final causes.

Practical and Non-Practical Reason

So far, in talking about reason, I have been saying things which I have hoped would be generally applicable to reason, or to reasons, or to reasoning, without attending to the possibility that the existence of importantly different kinds of reasoning might impose qualifications and, indeed, introduce asymmetries which should have been taken into account. In particular, I have been paying no detailed attention to the relation between practical and non-practical (or as I shall call it, borrowing an invention of von Wright, *alethic*) reason (or reasoning). It is time to remedy this omission.

Kant insisted that it is one and the same faculty of reason which issues in alethic reasoning and in practical reasoning. How one should individuate faculties and capacities is a mystery which is very much unfathomed, though it is not, I hope, unfathomable; so perhaps we might make things a little easier if, instead of asking whether Kant's view is correct, we were to ask whether the word 'reason' has the same meaning in the phrases 'alethic reason' and 'practical reason', or (alternatively) has different meanings which are related by a greater or lesser measure of analogy. The distinction just introduced between having a single meaning and having a plurality of meanings which are analogically related is, of course, far from clear; but perhaps it is clear enough for use in raising questions, even if it would need plastic surgery before being usable in solving them.[4] Most people (even philosophical people) would, I suspect, take the view that 'reason' has a single meaning in the two contexts, and there might be an even stronger consensus with regard to the answer to a parallel question about the word 'argument'. But, when we move to other words which seem to be very closely connected with reason, the situation seems to change. Kant (I suspect) would have been firmly in favour of the idea that the word 'necessary' (and its cognates) has the same meaning (or meanings) in the two sentences (1) "It is necessary for you to go to the hospital tomorrow" and (2) "It is necessary that the paper will ignite" (or a little more idiomatically "The paper will necessarily ignite"), said when someone is about to put a match to the paper; though he would of course have allowed that there are enormously important differences between the two sorts of statement. But, whether or not Kant would have taken this position, I am certain that there are many who would not; and the case is similar with other allied words. It is almost common form to suppose that there are (at least) two senses of the word 'ought', exhibited severally in the sentences (1) "You ought to get your hair cut" and (said several hours later, to someone else) (2) "His hair ought to be cut by now"; these are called (respectively) the practical and the epistemic 'ought'. And what of "The roof must have fallen in" and "The butler must repair the roof"? Or, "Spinoza should win the 3.30, so you should put your money on him"?

I shall approach the exploration of this rather ill-defined array of problems by way of a brief discussion of a fairly recent attempt to exhibit an analogy between a certain sort of practical argument and a certain sort of alethic argument. In "How is Weakness of the Will Possible?",[5] Donald Davidson offers a proposal which may be (with minor liberties) summarized as follows:

[4] For a discussion of the distinction, see Paul Grice, "Prolegomena", in *Studies in the Ways of Words* (Cambridge, Mass.: Harvard University Press, 1989), 3–21.]
[5] In Donald Davidson, *Essays on Actions and Events* (Oxford: Oxford University Press, 1980).]

(i) We should compare such sentences as

(1) Given that the barometer falls, it will probably rain tonight.

(2) Given that act *a* would be a lie and act *b* would not, *b* is better than *a*.

These may be regarded as exemplifying, respectively, the forms:

(1a) Prob (m_1; p) and

(2a) Pf (m_1; *b* better than *a*).[6]

(ii) The logical analogy between these two forms (between the two 'connectives') comes out in the *defeasible* nature of arguments in which such sentences as (1) and (2) occur. The forms

p& (if p, q)

p&r & (if p&r, not −q)

are inconsistent with one another; so an (ordinary deductive) inference from p& (if p, q) to q cannot be upset by the addition of a further true premiss. But the forms

(1aa) Prob (m_1; p) & m_1

(1ab) Prob (m_2; p) & m_2

(1ac) Prob (m_1 & m_2; p) & (m_1 & m_2)

may all be true together; so, while in certain circumstances the non-demonstrative argument:

Prob (m_1; p)

m_1
_____

p

will be acceptable, it will not be acceptable (even though its premisses are known to be true), if, for example, it is also known to be true that ((1ac)) Prob (m_1 & m_2; p), and also that m_1 & m_2. In parallel fashion, it will sometimes be proper to infer from (2) "Pf (Given that act *a* would be a lie and act *b* would not, *b* is better than *a*" together with "Act *a* would be a lie and act *b* would not" to "*b* is better than *a*"; but it will not be proper to infer to this conclusion if it is also known (for example) that act *a* would prevent a murder while act *b* would not.

[6 'Pf' is to be read as "prima facie".]

(iii) The defeasible character of such arguments requires that detachment should be subject to a "Principle of Total Evidence" (PTE), the precise nature of which need not concern us just at the moment. Nor, I may add, shall I here be concerned with the use which Davidson makes of the material just presented in his attempt to dispose of his version of the 'paradox' of incontinence, except to mention that the conclusions of practical arguments which may be reached under licence from a PTE (for example, 'b is better than a') are called by him unconditional value judgements, to distinguish them from the conditional, or prima facie, judgements from which they may be derived.

Now for some signs of discomfort. So far as I can see, Davidson's connective 'Pf', as distinct from 'Prob', is restricted in its occurrences; it can occur legitimately only in contextual conjunction with pairs of sentences, the second of which is of the form "b is better than a". This suggests that, as a first move, we might join 'Pf' and 'better' into a single ternary connective, preserving syntactical propriety by treating 'a' and 'b' not as stand-ins for action-*designators* (for example, "my telling a lie") but for action-*sentences* (for example, "I tell a lie"); and that as a second move we omit 'Pf', leaving ourselves with the simpler connective "better". We could (by a slight extension) then reach the following set of analogies:

"Prob (h; p)" as the analogue of "Good (h; a, b)"
"More prob (h; p, q)" as the analogue of "Better (h; a, b)".

The conditional/unconditional distinction would then be represented by the pair of distinctions between:

(1) (i) Better (h; b, a) and (ii) Better (b, a) and
(2) (i) Best (h; a) and (ii) Best (a).

But now a slightly disturbing asymmetry appears. According to Davidson, the conclusion sometimes to be reached by detachment from the pair of premisses "Prob (h; p)" and "h" is "p"; whereas the operation of detachment on (say) "Best (h; a)" and "h" cannot yield "a" (that is, "x does A") but has to yield "Best (a)" (that is, "it is best that x does A"); in practical arguments, unlike probabilistic arguments, the special connective (in our revised scheme) will not disappear in the conclusion. If we pursue the course on which I have embarked, and maintain zeal for the maximization of analogy, we should take the alethic analogue for "Best (a)" to be not "p", but "Prob (p)" (representing either "it is probable that p" or "Probably p"); a structure, that is, which does not appear in Davidson's scheme. If we are to find, on the practical side, an analogue for "p" other than "Best (a)", we shall have to devise one, since so far none is provided.

On the alethic side, then, given premisses of the forms "Prob (h, p)" and "h", one may, under licence, come to rest *either* with:

I (*a*) "Probably p" or (*b*) "it is probable that p"

or with

II "p".

We should not allow an excessive preoccupation with the maxim that probability is always relative to blind us to I(*a*) and I(*b*), or to prevent us from considering their relation to II, and to one another. If our present direction is correct, "It is best that I do A" emerges as the practical analogue for either I(*a*) or I(*b*); and the practical analogue for II is not hard to locate. If one function of probabilistic argument is to reach belief (that p), the corresponding function of practical argument should be to reach an intention or decision; and what should correspond to saying "p", as an expression of one's belief, is saying, "I shall do A", as an expression of one's intention or decision.

It seems to me that, at this point, Davidson might object to my procedure to date on two scores. *First*, a more recent paper[7] of his made it clear that (as I had long suspected) he wished to identify my intending to do A with my making (or accepting) an unconditional value judgement in favour of my doing A; that being so, he could hardly be expected to go along with my proposal to distinguish between "Best (a)" and "I shall do A". *My judging* that Best (a) would for him be what I report when I say "I shall do A". I have publicly advanced my objections to this account of intending,[8] and I shall not renew the battle, particularly as I am at the present moment using Davidson's paper more as a point of departure than as a target for attack. *Secondly*, it is possible that

[7 Davidson, in *Essays on Actions and Events*.]
[8 Grice, "Actions and Events".]

he (or someone else) might be troubled on the grounds that, once I allow "I shall do A" as a possible conclusion of a practical argument, I am licensing arguments as valid the conclusions of which cannot, or should not, be drawn by everyone who accepts their premisses. Suppose I have the premiss "Best that, if Tommy has been tormenting my cat, I ambush him on his way home from school"; I acquire also the premiss that Tommy has been tormenting my cat, together with a licence from the appropriate PTE; and I reach the conclusion (legitimately) that I shall ambush Tommy. My next-door neighbour hears me rehearsing this argument; he cannot, *logically*, draw (as an expression of *my* intention) the conclusion that I shall ambush Tommy; he cannot *decently* draw, as an expression of *his* intention, the conclusion that I shall ambush Tommy; and he cannot *sensibly* draw, as an expression of *his* intention, that *he* will ambush Tommy. The best he can do is to comment that I have reached the conclusion which it was proper for me to reach. This phenomenon, of course, arises from the fact (or seeming fact) that in the practical area what are reasons for one person to do something may not be reasons for another person to do that thing, nor indeed to do anything at all. To one who would look askance at such arguments as this, I would reply that it is more important to provide for the legitimization of expressions of intention as conclusions of valid arguments than to preserve a favoured dogma about the interpersonal character of argument. In suggesting this reply, however, I am not closing my eyes to the possibility that the feature under debate might at some point prove a source of trouble.

To return to my project. I wish to suggest not merely that such structures as Prob (h; p) and Best (h; a) are analogous, but that they can be replaced by more complex structures containing a common constant. There seems to me to be some linguistic support for this idea. As already noted, words like 'reason' and 'justification' operate in both the alethic and the practical domain. "There is every reason to regard him as a fool" is, semantically, not very different from "In all probability he is a fool"; and "There is every reason to fire him" is not very different from "It is best to fire him". Similar linguistic phenomena are to hand not only with respect to "justification" but also with respect to "ought" and "should". A further hint is provided by the behaviours of the phrase "it is to be expected". To say, "It is to be expected of a lawyer that he will earn $100,000 a year", though not wholly unambiguous, seems to be on one interpretation close to "A lawyer will probably earn $100,000 a year". To say, "It is to be expected of a lawyer that he earn $100,000 a year" seems, however, to be obstinately practical in sense; it is asserted (somewhat curiously, perhaps) that it is in some way or other incumbent on a lawyer to earn that not insignificant income. If we accept the idea that the difference between these two statements, which consists in the difference between the presence of the verb-phrase "will earn" and that of the verb-phrase "earn", is a difference of *mood*, then it looks as if a shift from alethic to practical discourse may be signalled by a shift in mood with respect to a subordinate verb.

An initial version of the idea I want to explore is that we represent the sentences (1) "John should be recovering his health by now" and (2) "John should join AA" as having the following structures; *first*, a common "rationality" operator 'Acc', to be heard as "it is reasonable that", "it is acceptable that", "it ought to be that", "it should be that", or in some other similar way; *next*, one or other of two mood-operators, which in the case of (1) are to be written as '⊢' and in the case of (2) are to be written as '!'; and finally a 'radical', to be represented by 'r' or some other lower-case letter. The structure for (1) is Acc + ⊢ + r, for (2) Acc + ! + r, with each symbol falling within the scope of its predecessor. I am thinking of a radical in pretty much the same kind of way as recent writers who have used that term (or the term 'phrastic'); I think of it as a sequence in the underlying structural representation of sentences, and I regard it as an undecided question whether there are any sentences in a natural language which contain a part which is a distinct surface counterpart of a radical (compare Wittgenstein's remarks about radicals in chemistry). Obviously the next topic for me to take up is the characterization of mood-operators.

Moods

There are in fact two connected questions on which I shall try to find something to say. *First*, there is the obvious demand for a characterization, or partial characterization, of mood-differences as they emerge in *speech* (which it is plausible to regard as their primary habitat); *second*, there is the question how, and to what extent, representations of moods, and so of mood-differences, which are suitable for application to speech may be legitimately imported into the representation of *thought*. We need to consider the second question, since, if the general 'rationality' operator is to signify something like acceptability, then the appearances of mood-operators within its scope will be proper only if they may properly occur within the scope of the psychological verb "accept".

The easiest way for me to expound my ideas on the first of these questions is by reference to a schematic table or diagram (see Fig. 2). I should at this point reiterate my temporary contempt for the use/mention distinction; my exposition would make the hair stand on end in the soul of a person specially sensitive in this area. But my guess is that the only historical philosophical mistake properly attributable to use/mention confusion is Russell's argument against Frege in "On Denoting", and that there are virtually always acceptable ways of eliminating disregard of the distinction in a particular case, though the substitutes are usually lengthy, obscure, and tedious.

I shall make three initial assumptions: (1) That I may avail myself of two species of acceptance, namely, J-acceptance and V-acceptance, which I shall, on occasion, call respectively "judging" and "willing". The latter pair of words are to be thought of as technical or semi-technical, though they will signify states which approximate to what we vulgarly call "thinking (that p)" and "wanting (that p)", especially in the senses in which we can speak of beasts as thinking or wanting something. I here treat 'judge' and 'will' (and 'accept') as primitives; their proper interpretation would be determined by their role in a psychological theory (or sequence of psychological theories) designed to account for the behaviours of members of the animal kingdom, at different levels of psychological complexity (some classes of creatures being more complex than others). (2) That, as I suggested in a published article (the exact title of which I always find it difficult to remember),[9] at least at the point at which,

---

[9 Grice, "Utterer's Meaning, Sentence-Meaning, and Word-Meaning", *Foundations of Language*, 4 (Aug. 1968), 225–48.]

(Main clause):

U to utter to H [a sentence of the form] $O_{P1} + p$

if ...

(Antecedent clause)

Operation Number	*(Preamble)*	*(Supplement)*	*(Differential)*	*(Content) (Radical)*	*(Operator)*	*(Mood-name)*
(1) A	U wills H judges U	[none]	judges	P	$\vdash_A$	Judicative$_A$ ('Indicative')
B		wills H	...	...	$\vdash_B$	Judicative$_B$ ('Indicative')
(2) A	....	[none]	wills	...	$!_A$	Volitive$_A$ ('Intentional')
B	....	wills H	...	...	$!_B$	Volitive$_B$ ('Imperative')
(3) A	....	[none]	wills ($\exists_1\alpha$) (U α judges	...	$?_A{\vdash}$	Judicative Interrogative
B	....	wills ($\exists_1\alpha$) (H	wills U α judges	...	$?_B{\vdash}$	Judicative Interrogative
(4) A	....	[non] wills	wills ($\exists_1\alpha$) (U α wills	...	$?_A!$	Volitive Interrogative$_A$
B	....	($\exists_1\alpha$) (H	wills U α wills	...	$?_B!$	Volitive Interrogative$_B$

Notes: Interrogatives: (i) Legitimate substituends for 'α' are 'positively' and 'negatively'; positively judging that p, and negatively judging that p is judging that not-p.

(ii) The 'uniquely existential' quantifier ($\exists_1\alpha$) is to be given a 'substitutional' interpretation.

(iii) If the differential is supplemented (as in a B case), the quantifier is 'dragged back', so as to appear immediately before 'H' in the supplement.

FIG. 2. Schema of procedure-specifiers for mood-operators

2. Reason and Reasons

in one's syntactico-semantical theory of a particular language, one is introducing mood-differences (and possibly earlier), the proper form to use is a specification of speech-procedures; such specifiers would be of the general form "For U (utterer) to utter φ if . . ." where the blank is replaced by the appropriate condition. (3) That since in the preceding scheme 'φ' represents a structure and not a sentence or open sentence, there is no guarantee that actual sentences in the language under treatment will contain perspicuous and unambiguous representations of their moods or sub-moods; an individual sentence may correspond to two (or more) mood-different structures; the sentence will then be structurally ambiguous (multiplex in meaning) and will have more than one reading.

The general form of a procedure-specifier for a mood-operator, as you will see from Fig. 2, involves a main clause (which comes first) and an "antecedent" clause, which follows "if". In the schematic representation of the main clause, "U" represents an utterer, "H" a hearer, "P" a radical; and "Op_i" represents that operator whose number is i; for example, "Op_{3a}" would represent Operator Number 3A, which (since '? ⊢' appears in the Operator column for 3A) would be $?_A$ ⊢. The antecedent clause consists of a sequence whose elements are a *preamble*, a *supplement* to a differential (which is present only in a B-type case), a *differential*, and a *radical*. The preamble, which is always present, is invariant, and reads "U wills (that) H judges (that) U . . .". The supplement, if present, is also invariant; and the idea behind its varying presence or absence is connected, in the first instance, with the Volitive Mood (see initial assumption (2) above). It seemed to me that the difference between ordinary expressions of intention (such as "I shall not fail" or "They shall not pass") and ordinary imperatives (Like "Be a little kinder to him") could be accommodated by treating each as a special sub-mood of a superior mood; the characteristic feature of the superior mood (Volitive) is that it relates to willing that p, and in one subordinate case (the Intentional case) the utterer is concerned to reveal to the hearer that he (the utterer) wills that p, while in the other subordinate case (Imperative), U is concerned to reveal to H that U wills that *H* will that p. (In each case, of course, it is to be presumed that willing that p will have its standard outcome, namely, the actualization of p.) It also seemed to me that

there is a corresponding distinction between two "uses" of ordinary indicatives; sometimes one is *declaring* or *affirming* that p,
one's intention being primarily to get the hearer to think that the
speaker thinks that p; while sometimes one is *telling* the hearer
that p, that is to say, hoping to get *him* to think that p. It is true
that in the case of indicatives, unlike that of volitives, there is no
pair of devices which would ordinarily be thought of as mood-
markers which serves to distinguish the sub-mood of an indicative sentence; the recognition of the sub-mood has to come from
context, from the vocative use of the name of H, from the presence
of a speech-act verb, or from a sentence-adverbial phrase (like
"for your information"). But I have already, in my initial assumptions, allowed for such a situation. This A/B distinction seemed
to me to be also discernible in interrogatives (of this, a little
more later).

The differentials are each associated with, and serve to distinguish, 'superior' moods (judicative, volitive) and, apart from one
detail in the case of interrogatives, are invariant between 'A' and
'B' sub-moods of the superior mood; they are merely unsupple-
mented or supplemented, the former for an 'A' sub-mood and the
latter for a 'B' sub-mood. The radical needs at this point (I hope)
no further explanation, except that it might be useful to bear in
mind that I have *not* stipulated that the radical for an 'intentional'
(Volitive$_A$) incorporate a reference to U ("be in the first person"),
nor that the radical for an 'imperative' (Volitive$_B$) incorporate a
reference of H ("be in the second person"); "They shall not pass"
is a legitimate intentional, as is "You shall not get away with it";
and "The sergeant is to muster the men at dawn" (said by a cap-
tain to a lieutenant) is a perfectly good imperative. I will give in
full two examples of actual specifiers derived from the schema shown
in Fig. 2.

(1) U to utter to H $\vdash_A$ p *if* U wills (that) H judges (that) U
     judges p.
(2) U to utter to H $!_B$ p *if* U wills that H judges that U wills
     that H wills that p.

Since, of the states denoted by differentials in the figure, only
judging that p and willing that p are, in my view, strictly cases of
acceptance that p, and the ultimate purpose of my introducing this

characterization of moods is to reach a general account of linguistic forms which are to be conjoined, according to my proposal, with an 'acceptability' operator, the first two numbered rows of the figure are (at most) what I shall have a direct use for. But since it is of some importance to me that my treatment of moods should be (and should be thought to be) on the right lines, I have added a partial account of interrogatives, and I shall say a little more about them.

(1) There are two varieties of interrogatives, 'Yes/No' interrogatives (for example, "Is his face clean?") and 'W' interrogatives ("Who killed Cock Robin?", "Where has my beloved gone?", "How did he fix it?"). The specifiers derivable from the schema will provide only for 'Yes/No' interrogatives, though the figure could be quite easily amended so as to yield a restricted but very large class of 'W' interrogatives; I shall in a moment indicate how this could be done.

(2) The distinction between Judicative and Volitive Interrogatives corresponds with the difference between cases in which a questioner is indicated as being, in one way or another, concerned to obtain *information* ("Is he at home?"), and cases in which the questioner is indicated as being concerned to settle a problem about what he is to *do* ("Am I to leave the door open?", "Is the prisoner to be released?", "Shall I go on reading?"). This difference is fairly well represented in English grammar, and much better represented in the grammars of some other languages.

(3) The A/B differences are (I think) not marked at all in English grammar. They are, however, often quite easily detectable. There is usually a recognizable difference between a case in which someone says, musingly or reflectively, "Is he to be trusted?" (a case in which the speaker might say that he was just *wondering*), and a case in which he utters the same sentence as an *enquiry*; similarly, we can usually tell whether someone who says "Shall I accept the invitation?" is just trying to make up his mind, or is trying to get advice or instruction from his audience.

(4) The employment of the variable '$\propto$' needs to be explained. I have borrowed a little from an obscure branch of logic, once (but maybe no longer) practised, called (I think) "proto-thetic" (why?), the main rite in which was to quantify over (or through)

connectives. '∝' is to have as its two substituents "positively" and "negatively", which may modify the verbs 'judge' and 'will'; negatively judging or negatively willing that p is judging or willing that not-p. The quantifier $(\exists_1 \propto) \ldots$ has to be treated substitutionally, as specified in note (ii). If, for example, I *ask* someone whether John killed Cock Robin (B case), I do not want him merely to will that I have a particular "Logical Quality" in mind which I believe to apply; I want *him* to have one of the "Qualities" in mind which he wants me to believe to apply. To meet this demand, supplementation must 'drag back' the quantifier.

(5) To extend the schema so as to provide specifiers for '*single*' W-interrogatives (that is, questions like "What did the butler see?" rather than questions like "Who went where with whom at 4 o'clock yesterday afternoon?"), we need just a little extra apparatus. We need to be able to superscribe a 'W' in each interrogative operator (for example, $?^W_A \vdash$, $?^W_B !$), together with the proviso that a radical which follows a superscribed operator must be an 'open' radical, which contains one or more occurrences of just *one* free variable. And we need what I might call a 'chameleon' variable 'λ', to occur only in quantifiers, so that $(\exists\lambda)$ Fx is to be regarded as a way of writing $(\exists x)$ Fx, while $(\exists\lambda)$ Fy is a way of writing $(\exists y)$ Fy. To provide specifiers for W-superscribed operators, we simply delete the appearances of '∝' in the specifier for the corresponding un-superscribed operator, inserting instead the quantifier $(\exists_1\lambda)$ ($\ldots$) at the position previously occupied by $(\exists_1 \propto)$ ($\ldots$). For example: the specifiers for "Who killed Cock Robin?" (used as an enquiry) would be: "U to utter to H '$?^W_B \vdash$: x killed Cock Robin' *if* U wills H to judge U to will that $(\exists_1\lambda)$ (H should will that U judges (x killed Cock Robin))"; in which '$(\exists_1\lambda)$' will "take on" the shape '$(\exists_1 x)$' since 'x' is the free variable within its scope.

Relativized and Absolute Modalities

I propose now to return,[10] for a closer look, to an objection which I have already remarked upon briefly, and in a none too exact

[10 Grice wrote this section in 1987–8; he added it to the material in this chapter simply at the end.]

2. *Reason and Reasons* 57

manner. In outline, the objection runs as follows. We find in the practical area, though not in the alethic area, non-trivial examples of relativization of particular modalities to individual persons; and the restructuring of such examples to the practical area bodes very ill for the contention that modalities are equivocal with respect to practical and alethic discussion. If they were, equivocal non-trivial relativization should appear either in both kinds of discourse or in neither. Let us expand this objection in relation to an example, not (seemingly) different from some already adduced. Suppose someone were to say, in perhaps appropriately fervent tones, "Richard Nixon must get the Oxford Chair of Moral and Pastoral Theology". Depending on context, one might find three different interpretations, all of them falling within the volitive zone. (A) One might mean that it is vital (perhaps vital to the world, or to some microcosm which is momentarily taken as if it were the world), that RN should be established in this position. On this interpretation, one would not be laying on any agent's shoulders an incumbency to see to it, that this happy state be realized, unless it were on the shoulders of someone with a reputation for total ineffectiveness in mundane affairs, like The Almighty. (B) On another interpretation, one would be invoking a supposed incumbency, perhaps an incumbency on 'us' (whoever 'us' might be) to secure the result. (C) On what might be a particularly natural interpretation, one would be charging *Richard Nixon* with an incumbency to secure his own election to this august chair. On both interpretations (B) and (C), one would be advancing the idea that it was necessary *relative to some potential agent* ('us' or RN) that RN obtain the chair. On the alethic side, no such *significant* relativity is observable. One might mean by uttering the sentence that (for example) it is a one-horse race (a shoe-in) for RN; but that kind of necessity would not be relativized, except perhaps timidly to any person whatsoever as something which he (like everyone else) would have to admit, or alternatively to some particular person whose view it is that RN cannot but be chosen (and this is not an interesting interpretation). A parallel phenomenon will (it may be alleged) be discernible with respect to the other modals, like 'ought' and 'should' and 'there is (a) reason to (for)'. Citation of such phenomenon might also be reinforced by the observation that, in a number of cases, there are special words which incorporate relativity into their meaning;

connected with the words 'necessary' and 'ought', there are such words as 'need' and 'obligation' which it is plausible to regard as exclusively volitive (practical) and especially relative in meaning. While the appearance of such specialized words in the language is not conclusive (it is notoriously difficult to find a procedure for distinguishing between the existence of a generic notion and the existence of a plurality of less generic notions related by analogy), the one-sidedness of relativization may well be held to be an obstacle in the Equivocality Thesis.

It seems to me that, initially, two main directions of reply present themselves: (A) it might be claimed that the one-sidedness of relativization, even if genuine or fundamental, is not damaging to the Equivocality Thesis;[11] or (B) it might be argued that the one-sidedness of relativization is only a surface phenomenon, in that the relativized volitive modalities can be represented as being derivable from ulterior absolute modalities, and so as being in principle eliminable. Let us take these up in turn.

(A) To see more clearly whether or not the admission of relativized modalities, even if one-sided, would damage the Equivocality Thesis, one might take a further look (this time in a slightly more formal way) at how such a thesis would be most securely established. It seems to me that it would be strong support for such a thesis if appropriate modal expressions could be introduced into a system of natural deduction, designed to handle both alethic and volitive moods, independently of any reference to the other constraints in such a system, and, in particular, independently of any reference to specific moods. We might hope to find, for each member of a certain family of modalities, an introduction rule and an elimination rule which would be analogous to the rules available for classical logical constants. Suggestions are not hard to come by. Let us suppose that we are seeking to provide such a pair of rules for the particular modality of *necessity*. For an *introduction* rule we might consider the following (I think equivalent) forms: (*a*) "If a sentence $\ulcorner\varphi\urcorner$ is demonstrable then $\ulcorner$Necessary$\urcorner$ is demonstrable; (*b*) "Provided $\ulcorner\varphi\urcorner$ is dependent on no assumptions, to derive $\ulcorner\varphi\urcorner$ from $\ulcorner$necessary $\varphi\urcorner$". For an *elimination* rule we might consider "From $\ulcorner$Necessary $\varphi\urcorner$ to derive $\ulcorner\varphi\urcorner$". It is to be under-

---

[11] See p. 90 for a statement of the Thesis.

stood, of course, that the values of the syntactical variable 'φ' would contain mood markers; both "⊢$\sqrt{}$the pig went to market"[12] and "!$\sqrt{}$the pig goes to market" would be proper substitutes for 'φ' but "$\sqrt{}$the pig goes to market" would not (unless we accept the idea that radicals are alethic sentences, mentioned in Chapter 3).

Of course, if we accept these suggestions, we shall also have to accept whatever uncomfortable consequences they may entail. In particular we shall have to meet the opposition of those who think, at least with respect to necessity, that there is a need to distinguish a semantic notion of *necessity/validity* from a syntactical, or partially syntactical, notion of *provability*. The grounds on which such a contention would be based might be a demand for a distinct notion of necessity by reference to which, in proofs of soundness or of completeness, the adequacy or strength of a particular notion of provability-in-a-system might be supported; or they might be the intuitively not unattractive idea that the non-provability and non-disprovability of some mathematician's thesis (say Fermat's conjecture), should the thesis be neither provable nor disprovable, would not prohibit the thesis (or its negation) from being necessary; we just might never know to which of them necessity attaches. Such questions as these plainly deserve study; but I myself have neither the time nor perhaps the competence to pursue them further, at this moment. The suggested elimination rule treats it as a general feature of necessity, holding across the board, that a statement about necessity entails the result of dropping the necessity operator; the use made of mood-operators allows the reversal of the standard idea that this feature attaches to (indicative) modal logic but not to deontic logic, since 'obligatory A' does not entail the truth of 'A'. With respect to this suggestion the salient problem will be one of interpretation once it is understood that 'φ' is not restricted to indicative mood-markers, but may cloak a volitive operator. What is it to mean to say that "Let it be that I eat my hat" is entailed by, or is derivable from, "It is necessary that let it be that I eat my hat" ("I must/have to eat my hat")? On the face of it two lines of interpretation seem to offer themselves: (i) to say that this derivability obtains is to say that one who says (thinks) "I must [have to] eat my hat" is committed to seeing (accepting) (cannot consistently refuse to accept) "let it be that I eat my hat" ("I shall

[12 Where φ is a sentence, $\sqrt{\varphi}$ is the radical contained in (or underlying) φ.]

(intentional) eat my hat"); (ii) that it is to say that if satisfactoriness (in this case truth) attaches to "It is necessary for me to eat
my hat", then satisfactoriness (in form of practical value) attaches
to "let me eat my hat" ("I shall (intentional) eat my hat"). I think
we are at liberty to adopt either of these lines.

The adoption of the proposal under discussion will also involve
further work in some other directions. I have sketched its application only to the idea of necessity; but there is, of course, a larger
class of modals, including not only "necessary", but "*ceteris
paribus*", "might", "probable", and so forth, to which the project
of characterization by means of a pair of rules (introducing and
eliminative) would have to be extended; and its extension might
not be plain sailing. And the centrepiece of the programme will
itself need some further elaboration. Can we be sure, for instance,
that the provision of such a pair of rules is sufficient for the unique
determination of a concept, or might it be that, while such concepts as those of modality require the availability of such pairs of
rules, more than one modal concept (or even more than one concept, not necessarily in every case modal) may be associated with
a single pair of rules, so that more than the provision of the rules
will be needed for a full discrimination of any one concept? How
are we to find out and justify the answer to such a question? And
what should be said of Pravity's conjecture (roughly) that the nature
of the introduction rule determines the character of the elimination rule? But these questions I shall now leave on one side, proceeding to more pressing matters.

I have so far made no mention of the fairly obvious fact that,
if the introduction rule for 'necessary' in effect bids us ascribe necessity to whatever is demonstrable, then necessity is essentially relative to a system or theory, since it is within systems or theories
that demonstration is achieved; and indeed is upon the constitution of the system or theory within which it is achieved that the
possibility of demonstration depends. So long as the parent system
is held invariant, reference to it may perhaps be safely omitted;
but if the reference-system is not invariant, and if such variation
carries with it variation in the type or dimension of necessity, then
anonymity in such reference can no longer be safely preserved. This,
I would suggest, is the situation which prevails; there are notorious different varieties of necessity—logical, metaphysical, physical,

psychological, moral, practical, legal and (why not?) even ichthyo-logical (perhaps); and, as I see things, each of these adverbs serves to indicate a more or less specific type of system or theory with references to which necessity (demonstrability) obtains.

Some of the consequences or likely developments of a position of this sort should not be ignored. (1) The idea of treating types of necessity as explicable by a reference to the theory or system which determines demonstrability will, in certain cases, lead to a reversal of the assumptions about priority which some philo-sophers would be inclined to make. Many, I suspect, would regard it as rational to suppose that what a logical theory (system) does is to systematize a corpus of antecedently given logical necessities, and (perhaps an even more natural supposition) that moral the-ory does (or would if there *were* such a theory) systematize antecedent given obligations or incumbencies. But the present proposal would disallow these modes of thinking. If incumbencies are moral necessities, and moral necessities are what is demonstrable in an (acceptable) moral theory or system, the system comes first and cannot be informatively characterized as this system relating to incumbencies or moral necessities. Similarly a logical theory must be characterizable otherwise than by reference to its concern with logical necessities. This reversal of direction I find appealing, particularly as it would emphasize the central importance of the construction of theories or systems; no system, no necessity.

There is no reason to expect that the various theories or systems by reference to which the general characterizations of modality, such as necessity, are to be diversified, will be either detached from or independent of each other. Rather one should expect to find serial relationships within groups of systems: theory A (say logic) is presupposed by theory B (say metaphysics), which in turn is pre-supposed by theory C (say physics), which in turn is presupposed by theory D (say physiology), in which we may expect to find our "theory-space" being stocked bit by bit with extensions of prior occupants thereof. But perhaps not *every* extension of a junior theory will give the (a new) adverbial with which to modify such modals as "necessary". I expect that there are special laws or gen-eralities which are common and peculiar to fish; but I would doubt whether this fact (if it be a fact) would give one a special type of necessity, namely, ichthyological necessity. It looks to me as if it may be the case that any theory which creates a further adverbial to modify 'necessary' must provide an extension of a certain degree or kind of generality, which ichthyology would fail to reach; though I have no idea how such two types or levels of generality should be characterized.

We may now ask whether these reflections about the relativity of necessity (and maybe other modalities) to theories or systems will aid us in the defence of the Equivocality Thesis against the threat seemingly presented by one-sided relativization of such modalities to persons. I think that they may, provided that we can represent any *personal* relativity sometimes exhibited by practical modals as *a special case* of relativity to a given system. Let us consider what the import of the relativization of a particular modal, say 'necessary' to an individual person or creature, might be. One interesting possibility is that the relativization indicates a person whose judgement or opinion it is that something or other is the case: "For Dr Keate, it is necessary that every boy should be beaten at least once a week." This case is an uninteresting in that this kind of relativity is not restricted to practical modals, nor indeed to *modals*; "for . . ." works as a sentence-adverbial ("For Dr Keate schoolboys are a species of reptile"). Three other more authentic cases of modality-relativization are also more interesting. The unidiomatic form "It is necessary with respect to Mrs Thatcher that Mr Heath become an ambassador at once" might be interpreted as saying (*a*) that it is Mrs Thatcher who has ordained this fate for Mr Heath, (*b*) that it is she to whose advantage it would be thus to dispose of Mr Heath, (*c*) that it is her business to see that the transformation is effected. Leaving on one side for a moment the by no means unimportant first alternative, we might perhaps put the second and third modes of interpretation to work. It is not too difficult to envisage a body of precepts about how to behave, relating to a single particular person, who is intended to be both agent and beneficiary with respect to the operation of these precepts; nor is it a great additional effort to suppose these precepts to be derivable from a limited number of parent precepts, still however retaining reference to the particular individual, and generally, with the aid of further factual premisses, a system which constitutes a self-help manual for that individual. It seems by no means out of the question that, if the references to that individual are to be irreducible (not eliminable in favour of references to classes of person to which the individual belongs), then the first interpretation might also have to be brought into play; the manual is a manual for a particular individual (and for no other individual) just because he has 'legislated' (rightly or wrongly) what his ends are to be. I am inclined to think of more or less articulated egoistic manuals of this sort as underlying morality.

We have now, I hope, reached the idea of relativized modalities as relating to establishability in a 'personalized system'. Let us see if the pattern of introduction/elimination rules can be extended to relativized necessity, regarded in this light. There seems to be no particular problem about allowing an introduction rule which tells us that, if it is established in X's 'personalized' system that φ, then ⌜it is necessary with respect to X that φ⌝ is true (establishable).

The accompanying elimination rule is, however, slightly less promising. If we suppose such a rule to tell us that, if one is committed to the idea that it is necessary with respect to X that φ, then one is also committed to whatever is expressed by φ, we shall be in trouble; for such a rule is not acceptable; φ will be a volitive expression such as "let it be that X eats his hat"; and *my* commitment to the idea that X's system requires him to eat his hat does not *ipso facto* involve *me* in accepting (volitively) "let X eat his hat". But if we take the elimination rule rather as telling us that, if it is necessary with respect to X that let X eat his hat, then "let X eat his hat" possesses satisfactoriness-with-respect-to-X, the situation is easier; for this version of the rule seems inoffensive. This interpretation of the elimination rule parallels the second option distinguished earlier, with respect to the form of the elimination rule for unrelativized necessity; so perhaps the deferred selection should be made, in favour of that option.

(B) But let us, without relying on the encouraging aspect of procedure (A), turn our attention to an assessment of the prospects of procedure (B), that is, to an attempt to exhibit the seeming one-sidedness of the appearance of relativity in modalities in the practical zone as an illusion, a surface phenomenon explicable in terms of absolute modalities. Considered in relation to necessity, the idea would be that to say (for example) "It is necessary for RN to apply for the Chair of M & P Theology" ("It is necessary relative to RN that let RN apply for the chair of M & P Theology") is merely to produce a specimen of conditional (hypothetical) necessity, a kind of necessity which is by no means confined to the practical (volitive) area. What is expressed by such an utterance can be represented as a consequence of a pair of premisses (*a*) "It is necessary that let anyone who satisfies condition C apply for a chair in M & P Theology" (when 'C' represents some possibly quite complex condition), and (*b*) "RN satisfies condition C"; indeed, if we allow ourselves to quantify over conditions (whatever they may be), we can represent its meaning by "There is a C such that it is necessary that let anyone who satisfies C apply for a chair in M & P Theology; and RN satisfies C"; this paraphrase uses no relativized modal, and (furthermore) is not importantly different in character from the proper expansion of the alethic "This bit of metal must dissolve in *aqua regia*" [being gold].

I very much doubt if this attempt to conjure away relativization from the concept of practical necessity can succeed. In the example under discussion, RN is spoken of as being *both* the person who is or should be *concerned* about what is being stated to be a matter of necessity, *and also* the agent (or patient) whose doings (or sufferings) are of concern. Often the same person operates (as here) in both roles; and where this is so, it is cosy to fall into the idea that a single reference to the agent (or patient) is all that is needed, and so that relativization can be eliminated. But things are not always thus; "It is necessary for (to) Joe Garagiola that the American public retains its interest in baseball" is different in this respect. So we need to distinguish between the person for whom something is a reason (or is necessary), and the person *about* whom we are talking when we say *what* is necessary, or what there is a reason for. Moreover, it seems plausible to suggest that, when no one is explicitly or implicitly referred to as a person for whom something is necessary (or as called for by reason), then the reason or the necessity is general (public or objective rather than private or subjective). The suggested treatment would represent it as of general concern that RN apply for the mentioned chair, which is quite inappropriate.[13] It may surely be a matter of personal

---

[13] See T. Nagel, *The Possibility of Altruism* (Oxford: Oxford University Press, 1970).

(private) necessity to RN that he apply for the chair, without it being a matter of proper concern to any other person that he so apply; and, while it is not clear exactly what kind or degree of intervention is sanctioned by a generally applicable (unrelativized) necessity, it is difficult to avoid the idea that some measure of intervention is justified (*ex vi termini*) in cases of such necessity.

The situation, already complex, is further complicated by a number of additional considerations. First, it might turn out to be the case that relativized necessities, though distinct from absolute necessities, can be backed or supported by absolute necessities. The private necessity in the case of RN, to apply for the chair, might be backed, in the first instance, by the ends which RN has, or has set for himself; but the adoption of these ends might not be arbitrary; there might be an acceptable generality affirming that for any one of a certain sort (which RN is) it is (or alternatively should be) a matter of private necessity to have these ends; and this generality might itself be a matter of some kind of necessity (alethic or practical). Private necessities would be distinct from, but possibly supported by, public necessities that in certain circumstances such private necessities should obtain. Again, the backing of private necessities by public necessities might be not just a feature which is sometimes present, but one which was in one way or another *demanded* (alethically or practically). It might be possible to argue for the acceptability of one or other of two "Universalizability Principles" relating to private (relativized) necessity:

(i) It is *factually* (alethically) necessary that, if it is necessary to someone X that p should be case [that let it be that p], then there is some condition S such that X satisfies and [necessarily] for anyone y who satisfies S, it is [practically] necessary for him (y) that let it be that p (that p should be the case);

(ii) It is *practically* necessary that, if it is necessary to someone X that p should be the case, then *let there be* some condition S, such that X satisfies S, and [necessarily] for anyone y who satisfies S, it is [practically] necessary for him (y) that let it be that p (that p should be the case).

Of these two principles, I must confess that I am attracted by the second, which makes it not a logical requirement, but so to speak a *rational desideratum* that one should accept something as a matter of practical necessity only if (and if) one can back its acceptance by a general principle about relativized necessity; this will allow people to be subject to real private necessities which are nevertheless not rationally well founded. But at this point we are, I think, just scratching the surface of a very difficult and very important philosophical area; much more attention to it is needed.

I have, in the present section, given a moderately strong green light to the idea (A) that the emergence of one-sided personal relativization in practical modalities would not damage the Equivocality Thesis, and a moderately strong red light to the idea (B) that such one-sided relativization is an illusion, to be dissolved into underlying absolute modalities. I would conclude this discussion with a brief mention of a third possibility (C), namely, that relativization is real, but is *not* one-sided but *two-sided*, being found on the alethic side as well as the volitive (practical). Along these lines one might seek to treat the possession of *essential* properties (for example, perhaps the possession by a *particular* table of the property of being made of wood) as analogous to relativized practical necessities; it is perhaps essential to the existence of *this* table that it may be made of wood (a table not made of wood could not be *this* table), analogous to the way in which it might be (in a practical case) essential to the existence of a particular human being (RN) that he breathe and perform other vital human functions. But further discussion of this idea would belong to an occasion in which the notions of life, purpose, and final causes are under examination.

3

Practical and Alethic Reasons: Part I

Introduction

Given the verbal (though I hope not conceptual) complexity of certain parts of the last chapter, particularly of the account of what I called moods and mood-operators, and in order to make the programme clearer, I shall begin this chapter by clarifying the programme. It seemed to me that the faculty of Reason is most closely connected (*a*) with Reasoning and (*b*) with Reasons. Reasons (justificatory) are the stuff of which reasoning is made, and reasoning may be required to arrive (in some cases) even at the simplest of reasons; so it seemed proper to proceed from a consideration of reasoning to a consideration of reasons.

(1) I distinguished three types of case (if you like, three ways of using the word) with respect to the word 'reason' ('reasons'), which I called the *explanatory* use (case), the *justificatory* use (case), and the *justificatory–explanatory* use (case), which I shall now rename the '*personal*' use (case). They are interconnected, and a prominent way in which they are interconnected is the following: if someone thinks that a certain set of considerations is a *justificatory* reason for doing, intending, or believing something, and if he in fact does, intends, or believes that thing because he so thinks, then his *personal* reason for actually doing (intending, believing) that thing is that the aforementioned set of considerations obtain; and to state that someone did (intended, believed) something for a specified *personal* reason is a special case of giving an *explanatory* reason for his doing (intending, believing) that thing.
(2) Since *justificatory* reasons, in the above sense, lie at the heart (so to speak) of reasons of other varieties, it seems proper to consider further the character of justificatory reasons. These are (or

are widely thought to be) divisible into practical and non-practical (alethic) reasons. It is plain that certain common words like 'must', 'ought', 'should', 'necessary', etc. (which I shall label 'common modals') not only are widely used in the specification of justificatory reasons in a way which is intimately connected with their justificatory character, but also are used on *both* sides of the practical/alethic barrier. It seems relevant, then, to ask whether common modals are univocal across this barrier (whether, that is, the barrier enforces changes of sense, or whether whatever multiplicities of sense these words may have appear equally on both sides of the barrier); or whether, on the other hand, there are merely *analogies* between the practical and alethic employments of common modals. This problem seems highly germane to Kant's claim that there is a single faculty of Reason.

(3) This question (or group of questions) about the possible indifference, with respect to their meaning, of common modals to crossing the barrier is in more ways than one a far from clear question. With the idea of making it somewhat clearer, while at the same time gaining some illumination about relations between practical and alethic reasons, I proposed to start (using as a springboard a suggestion of Davidson's) by explaining the possibility of giving a structural representation of sentences involving two modals, which seemingly inhabit opposite sides of the barrier (namely, "probable" and "desirable"), in terms of a single (maybe to some degree artificial) modal "it is acceptable that" in combination with one or other of two mode-markers, '⊢' and '!' followed by a phrastic (radical). (I propose, however, not to restrict myself indefinitely to this case, and to bring other common modals into the account.)

(4) I am in this chapter talking about 'modes' rather than 'moods' to make it clear that I am not trying to characterize what linguists would be likely to call 'moods' (though I would expect there to be important links between their 'moods' and my 'modes'). I would justify (or explain) my use of the term 'mode' by reference to my views about meaning. According to these views, *what a speaker means* is to be explained in terms of the effect which he intends to produce in an actual or possible hearer; and *what a sentence in a language means* is to be explained in terms of directives with respect to the employment of that sentence, in a primitive (basic) way, with a view to inducing in a hearer a certain kind of

effect; what a speaker means will very often differ from what the sentence which he uses means, but what he means would (or should) be discernible on the basis of knowing the directive for the sentence together with facts about the circumstances and intentions of the speaker. The intended effect on a hearer is (in my view) one or other of a set of psychological attitudes with respect to some 'propositional content' (to borrow momentarily a phrase which I do not normally use), and my mode-markers each correspond with one element in this set of attitudes (or set of 'modes of thinking').

With respect to a particular sentence of the form 'Op + R' (mode-marker + phrastic), I imagine the appropriate directive as arrived at in the following way. We have, *in the first instance*, a 'signification-system' S, which will enable us to reach, for R, a statement to the effect that R signifies that such-and-such; this may be taken as giving a specification of a 'factivity'-condition (more loosely, truth-condition) for R. To be handled by S_1, R may be of any degree of logical complexity, but is to be *pure* (free from embedded mode-markers). The meaning-specification for the particular sentence (Op + R) will then (in effect) be a directive to utter this sentence if you want to induce in a hearer the attitude corresponding to 'Op' (the mode-marker) with respect to that which R signifies (according to system S_1). Sentences thus provided for will have, in their structures, a *single* mode-marker with maximal scope (no embedding of such markers). However, it may be possible, *in the second instance*, to *extend* S_1 by setting up S_2 (containing S_1) which *does* allow for at least limited embedding of mode-markers. The idea which I am exploring relates to just such an extension. (I should perhaps remark that, though I am using, for my present purpose, a fairly standard idea of a 'radical' ('phrastic'), I am by no means free from qualms about it, as will appear shortly.) To return to the most directly relevant issues, my idea is that an examination of justificatory reasons leads naturally to an examination of modals (expressing specific kinds of justification) and mode-markers, which are intimately connected with psychological attitudes needing justification.

(5) The stages through which, on this occasion, I shall conduct my exploration of the idea which I proposed in paragraph (3) are as follows:

(A) a partial characterization of mode-markers as used in (or underlying) *speech*; this stage I virtually completed in the last chapter;

(B) a brief consideration of what modifications might be required or convenient for the employment of mode-markers in the representation of the content of *thought* (of acceptance);

(C) the application of the idea to be explored to a certain class of alethic acceptability statements (including certain probability statements) and to a certain class of practical acceptability statements, namely, *a class roughly corresponding to Kant's Technical Imperatives*. Then, some reflections on the capability of the initial idea to accommodate the extension of our consideration of practical acceptabilities to:

(D) prudential acceptabilities, and

(E) moral or Categorical acceptabilities. (The connections with Kant are obvious.) Finally, if we survive to that point,

(F) some attempt to assess the progress with respect to the "Univocality Question".

I shall in this chapter nearly finish my discussion of topic C, leaving the remaining topics until later. So I shall be lurching uncertainly in the general direction of Logic, while in the next chapter I shall be meandering gently in the suburbs of Morals.

(6) (Footnote) In discussing the Univocality Question, we should be careful, so far as is possible, to distinguish between differences in the semantic features of practical and alethic discourse which are attributable simply to differences between the two kinds of mode-marker (alethic and practical), and those which are not so attributable, or though so attributable do nevertheless indicate a failure of Univocality (or of equal Multivocality) on the part of the common modals. We know, of course, *in advance*, that the mode-markers are going to be importantly different, because of the difference of direction of fit obtaining between alethic and practical discourse; primitive (perceptual) beliefs may be roughly thought of as generated by states of the world, and so serve as checks on the acceptability of more sophisticated beliefs; whereas will *primarily* affects the world (rather than vice versa), and there is no factual check on the acceptability of volitions parallel to that

on the acceptability of beliefs. This difference, I think, is one which enormously impressed Kant.

My second main question with regard to modes is whether it is legitimate to apply devices, which are initially presented as structural elements underlying mode-differences expressed in *speech*, to the representation of the content of thought, and in particular of the content of *acceptance*-in-thought.

(1) Since our concern is now with thought and not with utterance, and since we are concerned to provide directives not about *how* to think, but rather about how to specify *what* we think, it will plainly be appropriate to substitute a thought-verb for the phrase "to utter to H" in the main clause of the schema. The verb "accept" would obviously be a proper substituend; but we may note with interest that the verb "think" itself (if regarded as a maximally general content-governing thought-verb) would also be appropriate since the specific mode of thinking involved (whether a species of acceptance or not) would be identified by the particular mode-operator; "think" would also have the advantage of generality. So the main clause will now read "x accepts (thinks) Op + p".

Since thinking, unlike conversation, is, in the crudest sense, at least, a one-party game, to retain as the preamble of the antecedent clause "x wills x judges x . . ." would be perverse; to consider the simplest of relevant cases, it is difficult indeed for me to think of occasions on which "I wanted myself to think that I thought that p" would be a happy description of my state. So let the revised preamble simply consist of "x". Our whole enterprise might seem to be fruitless if we did not allow the following specifiers:

(1) x accepts (thinks) $\vdash_A$ + p if (indeed iff, perhaps) x judges p
(2) x accepts (thinks) $!_A$ + p if (iff) x wills p.

But what about the two 'B' cases? Quite apart from cases in which it is my will *now* that I should judge or will p on some *future* occasion (cases which may exist, but which are not particularly relevant to my present purposes), there are important cases in which I will *now* that I judge or will *now* (or next to now) that p. These are cases in which my lower nature interferes; inclinations, or some other disturbing factors, stop me from judging or willing that p, but do not stop me from willing that I will or judge that p, a higher-order state which may or may not in the end win out. Such cases of incipient incontinence of will or judgement are endemic to the constitution of a rational being. It seems to me, then, that the 'B' cases should be allowed. Since, however, my present prime concern is with acceptability rather than with acceptance, and since it seems that what would justify accepting $\vdash_A$ p (or $!_A$ p) would also justify accepting $\vdash_B$ p (or $!_B$ p), and, again, vice versa, I think we can, within the scope of "it is acceptable that", safely omit the subscripts.

(2) A curious phenomenon comes to light. I began by assuming (or stipulating) that the verbs 'judge' and 'will' (acceptance-verbs) are to be 'completed' by *radicals* (phrastics). Yet when the machinery developed above has been applied, we find that the verb 'accept' (or 'think') is to be completed by something of the form 'Op + p', that is, by a *sentence*. Perhaps we might tolerate this syntactical ambivalence; but if we cannot, the remedy is not clear. It would, for example, not be satisfactory to suppose that 'that', when placed before a *sentence*, acts as a 'radicalizer' (is a functor expressing a function which takes that sentence on to its radical); for that way we should lose the differentiations effected by varying mode-markers, and this would be fatal to the scheme. This phenomenon certainly suggests that the attempt to distinguish radicals from sentences may be misguided; that if radicals are to be admitted at all, they should be identified with indicative sentences. The operator '$\vdash$' would then be a 'semantically vanishing' operator. But this does not wholly satisfy me; for, if '$\vdash$' is semantically vacuous, what happens to the subordinate distinction made by 'A' and 'B' markers, which seems genuine enough? We might find these markers 'hanging in the air', like two smiles left behind by the Cheshire Cat.

Whatever the outcome of this debate, however, I feel fairly confident that I could accommodate the formulation of my discussion to it.

Fuller Exposition of the 'Initial Idea'

First, some preliminary points. To provide at least a modicum of intelligibility for my discourse, I shall pronounce the judicative operator 'ᅡ' as 'it is the case that', and the volitive operator '!' as 'let it be that'; and I shall pronounce the sequence 'φ, ψ' as 'given that φ, ψ'. These vocal mannerisms will result in the production of some pretty barbarous 'English sentences'; but we must remember that what I shall be trying to do, in uttering such sentences, will be to represent supposedly underlying structure; if that is one's aim, one can hardly expect that one's speech-forms will be such as to excite the approval of, let us say, Jane Austen or Lord Macaulay. In any case, less horrendous, though (for my purposes) less perspicuous, alternatives will, I think, be available.

Further, I am going to be almost exclusively concerned with alethic and practical arguments, the proximate conclusions of which will be, respectively, of the forms 'Acc (ᅡ p)' and 'Acc (! p)'; for example, 'acceptable (it is the case that it snows)' and 'acceptable (let it be that I go home)'. There will be two possible ways of reading the latter sentence. We might regard 'acceptable' as a sentential adverb (modifier) like 'demonstrably'; in that case to say or think 'acceptable (let it be that I go home)' will be to say or think 'let it be that I go home', together with the qualification that what I say or think is acceptable; as one might say, 'acceptably, let it be that I go home'. To adopt this reading would seem to commit us to the impossibility of incontinence; for since 'accept that let it be that I go home' is to be my rewrite for 'V-accept (will) that I go home', anyone x who concluded, by practical argument, that 'acceptable let it be that x go home' would *ipso facto* will to go home. Similarly (though less paradoxically) any one who concluded, by alethic argument, 'acceptable it is the case that it snows', would *ipso facto* judge that it snows. So an alternative reading 'it is acceptable that let it be that I go home', which does not commit the speaker or thinker to 'let it be that I go home', seems preferable. We can, of course, retain the distinct form 'acceptably, let it be that (it is the case that) p' for renderings of 'desirably' and 'probably'.

Let us now tackle the judicative cases. I start with the assumption that arguments of the form 'A, so probably B' are sometimes (informally) valid; 'he has an exceptionally red face, so probably he has high blood pressure' might be informally valid, whereas 'he has an exceptionally red face, so probably he has musical talent' is unlikely to be allowed informal validity.

We might re-express this assumption by saying that it is sometimes the case that A informally yields-with-probability that B (where
'yields' is the converse of 'is inferable from'). If we wish to construct a form of argument the acceptability of which does not depend
on choice of substituends for 'A' and 'B', we may, so to speak, allow
into the object-language forms of sentence which correspond to
meta-statements of the form: 'A yields-with-probability that B'; we
may allow ourselves, for example, such a sentence as "it is probable, given that he has a very red face, that he has high blood pressure". This will provide us with the argument-patterns:

"Probable, given A, that B

    <u>A</u>

so probably, B"

or

"Probable, given A, that B

    <u>A</u>

so, probable that B".

To take the second pattern, the legitimacy of such an inferential
transition will not depend on the identity of 'A' or of 'B', though
it *will* depend (as was stated in the previous chapter) on a licence
from a suitably formulated 'Principle of Total Evidence'.

The proposal which I am considering (in pursuit of the 'initial
idea') would (roughly) involve rewriting the second pattern of argument so that it reads:

It is acceptable, given that it is the case that A, that it is the case
that B.

It is the case that A.

To apply this schema to a particular case, we generated the particular argument:

It is acceptable, given that it is the case that Snodgrass has a red
face, that it is the case that Snodgrass has high blood pressure.

It is the case that *Snodgrass has a red face*.

So, it is acceptable that it is the case that Snodgrass has high
blood pressure.

If we make the further assumption that the singular 'conditional' acceptability statement which is the first premiss of the above argument may be (and perhaps has to be) reached by an analogue of the rule of universal instantiation from a general acceptability statement, we make room for such *general* acceptability sentences as:

> It is acceptable, given that it is the case that x has a red face, that it is the case that x has high blood pressure.

which are of the form "It is acceptable, given that it is the case that Fx, that it is the case that Gx'; 'x' here is, you will note, an unbound variable; and the form might also (loosely) be read (pronounced) as: "It is acceptable, given that it is the case that one (something) is F, that it is the case that one (it) is G." All of this is (I think) pretty platitudinous; which is just as well, since it is to serve as a model for the treatment of practical argument.

To turn from the alethic to the practical dimension. Here (the proposal goes) we may proceed, in a fashion almost exactly parallel to that adopted on the alethic side, through the following sequence of stages:

(1) Arguments (in thought or speech) of the form:

Let it be that A

It is the case that B

so, with some degree of desirability, let it be that C

are sometimes (and sometimes not) informally valid (or acceptable).

(2) Arguments of the form:

It is desirable, given that let it be that A and that it is the case that B, that let it be that C

Let it be that A

It is the case that B

so, it is desirable that let it be that C

should, therefore, be allowed to be formally acceptable, subject to licence from a Principle of Total Evidence.

(3) In accordance with our proposal such arguments will be rewritten:

It is *acceptable*, given that let it be A and that it is the case that
B, that let it be that C

Let it be that A

It is the case that B

so, it is desirable that let it be that C

(4) The first premisses of such arguments may be (and perhaps
have to be) reached by instantiation from general acceptability statements of the form: "It is acceptable, given that let one be E and
that it is the case that one is F, that let it be that one is G." We
may note that sentences like "it is snowing" can be trivially recast
so as (in effect) to appear as third premisses in such arguments
(with 'open' counterparts inside the acceptability sentence; they can
be rewritten as, for example, "Snodgrass is such that it is snowing"). We are now in possession of such exciting general acceptability sentences as: "It is acceptable, given that let it be that one
keeps dry and that it is the case that one is such that it is raining,
that let one take with one one's umbrella."

(5) A special subclass of general acceptability sentences (and of
practical arguments) can be generated by 'trivializing' the predicate in the judicative premiss (making it a 'universal predicate'). If,
for example, I take 'x is F' to represent 'x is identical with x' the
judicative sub-clause may be omitted from the general acceptability
sentence, with a corresponding 'reduction' in the shape of the related
practical argument. We have therefore such argument sequences
as the following:

(P_i) It is acceptable, given that let it be that one survives, that
let it be that one eats

So (by U_i) It is acceptable, given that let it be that Snodgrass
survives, that let it be that Snodgrass eats

(P_2) Let it be that Snodgrass survives

So (by Det) It is acceptable that let it be that Snodgrass eats.

We should also, at some point, consider further transitions to:

(*a*) Acceptably, let it be that Snodgrass eats,

and to:

(*b*) Let it be that Snodgrass eats.

And we may also note that, as a more colloquial substitute for "Let it be that one (Snodgrass) survives (eats)" the form "one (Snodgrass) is to survive (eat)" is available; we thus obtain prettier inhabitants of antecedent clauses, for example, "given that Snodgrass is to survive".

We must now pay some attention to the varieties of acceptability statement to be found within each of the alethic and practical dimensions; it will, of course, be essential to the large-scale success of the proposal which I am exploring that one should be able to show that for every such variant within one dimension there is a corresponding variant within the other. Within the area of defeasible generalizations, there is another variant which, in my view, extends across the board in the way just indicated, namely, the *unweighted* acceptability generalization (with associated singular conditionals), or, as I shall also call it, the *ceteris paribus* generalization. Such generalization I take to be of the form "It is acceptable (*ceteris paribus*), given that ϕX, that ψX" and I think we find both practical and alethic examples of the form; for example, "It is *ceteris paribus* acceptable, given that it is the case that one likes a person, that it is the case that one wants his company", which is not incompatible with "It is *ceteris paribus* acceptable, given that it is the case that one likes a person and that one is feeling ill, that one does not want his company". We also find "It is *ceteris paribus* acceptable, given that let it be that one leaves the country and given that it is the case that one is an alien, that let it be that one obtains a sailing permit from Internal Revenue", which is compatible with "It is *ceteris paribus* acceptable, given that let it be that one leaves the country and given that it is the case that one is an alien and that one is a close friend of the President, that let it be that one does not obtain a sailing permit, and that one arranges to travel in Air Force I".

I discussed this kind of generalization, or 'law', briefly in "Method in Philosophical Psychology"[1] and shall not dilate on its features here. I will just remark that it can be adapted to handle 'functional laws' (in the way suggested in that address), and that

[1] Paul Grice, "Method in Philosophical Psychology", *Proceedings and Addresses of the American Philosophical Association*, 48 (Nov. 1975), 23–53.]

it is different from the closely related use of universal generaliza-tions in 'artificially closed systems', where some relevant parameter is deliberately ignored, to be taken care of by an extension to the system; for in that case, when the extension is made, the original law has to be modified or corrected, whereas my *ceteris paribus* generalization can *survive* in an extended system; and I regard this as a particular advantage to philosophical psychology.

In addition to these two *defeasible* types of acceptability gener-alization (each with alethic and practical sub-types), we have *non-defeasible* acceptability generalizations, with associated singu-lar conditionals, exemplifying what I might call 'unqualified', 'un-reserved', or 'full' acceptability claims. To express these I shall employ the (constructed) modal 'it is fully acceptable that . . .'; and again there will be occasion for its use in the representation both of alethic and of practical discourse. We have, in all, then, three varieties of acceptability statement (each with alethic and practical sub-types), associated with the modals "It is *fully* acceptable that . . ." (non-defeasible), 'it is *ceteris paribus* acceptable that . . .', and 'it is to such-and-such a degree acceptable that . . .', both of the latter pair being subject to defeasibility. (I should re-emphasize that, on the practical side, I am so far concerned to represent only statements which are analogous with Kant's Technical Imperatives ('Rules of Skill').)

I am now visited by a temptation, to which of course I shall yield, to link these varieties of acceptability statement with common modals; however, to preserve a façade of dignity I shall mark the modals I thus define with a *star*, to indicate that the modals so defined are only *candidates* for identification with the com-mon modals spelled in the same way. I am tempted to introduce 'it must* be that' as a modal whose sense is that of 'It is fully acceptable that' and 'it ought* to be that' as a modal whose sense is that of 'It is *ceteris paribus* (other things being equal) accept-able that'; for degree-variant acceptability I can think of no appealing vernacular counterpart other than 'acceptable' itself. After such introduction, we could allow the starred modals to become idiomatically embedded in the sentences in which they occur; as in "A bishop must* get fed up with politicians", and in "To keep his job, a bishop ought* not to show his irritation with politicians".

But I now confess that I am tempted to plunge even further into conceptual debauchery than I have already; having just, at considerable pains, got what might turn out to be common modals *into* my structures, I am at once inclined to get them out again. For it seems to me that one might be able, without change of sense, to employ forms of sentence which eliminate reference to acceptability, and so do not *need* the starred modals. One might be able, to this end, to exploit "if-then" conditionals (NB 'if . . . then', not just 'if') together with suitable modifiers. One might, for example, be able to re-express "A bishop must* get fed up with politicians" as "*If* one is a bishop, then (unreservedly) one will get fed up with the politicians"; and "To keep his job, a bishop ought* not to show his irritation with politicians" as "If one is to keep one's job and if one is a bishop, *then*, other things being equal, one is not to show one's irritation with politicians". Of course, when it comes to applying detachment to corresponding singular conditionals, we may need to have some way of indicating the character of the generalization from which the detached singular non-conditional sentence has been derived; the devising of such indices should not be beyond the wit of man. So far as generalizations of these kinds are concerned, it seems to me that one needs to be able to mark five features:

(1) conditionality;
(2) generality;
(3) type of generality (absolute, *ceteris paribus*, etc., thereby, *ipso facto*, discriminating with respect to defeasibility or indefeasibility);
(4) mode;
(5) (not so far mentioned) whether or not the generalization in question has or has not been derived from a simple enumeration of instances; because of their differences with respect to direction of fit, any such index will do real work in the case of alethic generalities, not in the case of practical generalities.

So long as these features are marked, we have all we need for our purposes. Furthermore, they are all (in some legitimate and intelligible sense) *formal* features, and indeed features which might be regarded as, in some sense, 'contained in' or 'required by' the concept of a rational being, since it would hardly be possible to engage in any kind of reasoning without being familiar with them. So, on the assumption that the starred modals are identifiable with their unstarred counterparts, we would seem to have reached the following positions.

(1) We have represented practical and alethic generalizations, and their associated conditionals, and with them certain common modals such as 'must' and 'ought', under a single notion of acceptability (with specific variants).

(2) We have decomposed acceptability itself into formal features.

(3) We have removed mystery from the alleged logical fact that acceptable practical 'ought' statements have to be derivable from an underlying generalization.

(4) Though these achievements (if such they be) might indeed not *settle* the 'univocality' questions, they can hardly be irrelevant to them.

I suspect that, if we were to telephone the illustrious Kant at his Elysian country club in order to impart to him this latest titbit of philosophical gossip, we might get the reply, "Big deal! Isn't that what I've been telling you all along?"

Principle of Total Evidence

I must now give a little attention to the matter of formulating an appropriate version of a "Principle of Total Evidence" (PTE), designed to govern detachment. I cannot expect to reach anything better than an approximation to an adequate formulation; but perhaps even that would be a help.

I shall start with weight-bearing alethic acceptability-conditionals (singular probability conditionals) and at once two remarks are called for: first, that I am no kind of expert in the theory of probability, so I shall say little and say it fast. Second, that the example I select will not be fully representative of reasoning in this area; but perhaps it will be good enough for present purposes.

S (subject) owns a firm which makes and sells ornaments constructed from seashells, and S is concerned, at t, to estimate whether the firm's business will improve during the coming year. S reflects that, these days, every beachcomber is collecting seashells like mad so as to sell them to firms such as his, so he can get seashells more cheaply; so it is likely, given that he will get seashells more cheaply, that the business will improve. He also reflects that his not easily replaceable craftsmen are getting restive for higher pay, and that he may have to give in; so he accepts that, given that the craftsmen are restive, that the business will not improve. He further reflects that ornaments from seashells are all the rage at the moment, so he may be able to put his prices up and make more money. He now consolidates these reflections and judges that it is 'pretty likely, given that he will get seashells more cheaply, that his employees are restive, and that everyone is eager to buy seashell ornaments, that his business will improve'. He now searches further to see if he can find any considerations which, when added to the antecedent of his last judgement, would result in an acceptable conditional favouring the supposition that his business will not improve. After due search, he fails to find any such disturbing consideration; so he 'detaches' and judges that it is pretty likely that his business will improve.

The salient points here are (1) that, by consolidation (compounding antecedents) of prior acceptability-conditionals, S has reached, by time t, an alethic acceptability-conditional which he accepts, and the antecedent of which he accepts. (2) That after due (proper) search for an 'upsetting' ('disturbing') conditional he has, by time t, failed to come up with one. Let me introduce two simple bits of terminology. Let us say that ψ is an *extension* of an antecedent ϕ if ψ is either identical with ϕ or is a further specification of ϕ; and let us say that the antecedent of a weighted acceptability-conditional C *favours* the consequent of C just in case the weight specified in C is above an indifference point (for example, assigns *probability* rather than *improbability*).

I will now attempt to formulate a version of a PTE (applicable to alethic acceptability-conditionals):

If (a) S accepts at t an alethic acceptability-conditional C_1, the antecedent of which favours, to degree d, the consequent of C_1,

   (b) S accepts at t the antecedent of C_1,

(*c*) after due search by S for such a (further) conditional, there is no conditional C_2 such that

  (1) S accepts at t C_2 and its antecedent,

  and (2) the antecedent of C_2 is an extension of the antecedent of C_1,

  and (3) the consequent of C_2 is a rival (incompatible with) of the consequent of C_1,

  and (4) the antecedent of C_2 favours the consequent of C_2 more than it favours the consequent of C_1:

then S may judge (accept) at t that the consequent of C_1 is acceptable to degree d.

For convenience, we might abbreviate the complex clause (C) in the antecedent of the above rule as 'C_1 is optimal for S at t'; with that abbreviation, the rule will run: "*If* S accepts at t an alethic acceptability-conditional C_1, the antecedent of which favours its consequent to degree d, and S accepts at t the antecedent of C_1, and C_1 is optimal for S at C_1, *then* S may accept (judge) at t that the consequent of C_1 is acceptable to degree d."

Before moving to the practical dimension, I have some observations to make.

(1) I have said here nothing about the initial establishment of weighted acceptability-generalizations (from which singular acceptability-conditionals may be derived by instantiation) nor about how to compound them. These are important and difficult questions, but lie outside my immediate purpose.

(2) I have been treating an instantiation step from such generalizations to related singular conditionals as 'automatic', reserving the application of detachment to those conditionals as what is subject to a version of PTE. But I can imagine someone taking the position that detachment is to be automatic, and that what is to be licensed by some version of PTE is the instantiation step. Obviously, for such a person, a differently formulated version of PTE would be needed.

(3) (Importantly) As I have set things up, an inferential licence to detach is relative to a subject (reasoner) S *and* to a particular time t. I am inclined to regard this feature of such rules as characteristic of defeasible inference.

(4) (Importantly) The application of my rule involves a *value-judgement*: it has to be determined or supposed by S that detachment does follow upon *due* or *proper* search for a 'disturbing' conditional. While I do not have to seek to characterize such a search more precisely, I do not regard this feature of my rule with distaste.

I now introduce an example from the practical dimension; it has, I must allow, at certain points a quaintness which might suggest that the whole philosophical story is not yet being told.

S is invited by his mother to visit her in Milwaukee next week. At this point he accepts the practical acceptability-conditional, which for simplicity I will formulate without (insertible) references to degree of acceptability. The conditional is: "It is acceptable, given that let S give his mother pleasure, and that S is her favourite son, that let S visit her in Milwaukee next week."

He reflects, and comes up with the following conditional (based on the fact that his firm is about to do its accounts, and he is head accountant): "It is acceptable, given that let S get ready the firm's accounts and that S is head accountant and it is accounting time, that let S spend next week in his office in Redwood City."

He compounds, and comes up with: "It is acceptable, *given* that let S give his mother pleasure and let S get ready the firm's accounts, and that S is her favourite son and S is head accountant and now is accounting time, *that* S visit his mother in Milwaukee for a long weekend and return to his office in Redwood City on Tuesday."

S is then suddenly reminded that his wife, Matilda, has just had a bad car accident and is lying in hospital in Boise, Idaho, with two broken legs and internal injuries. This prompts him to form the further judgement: "It is acceptable, *given* that let S sustain Matilda and that S is her husband and she is lying in Boise, Idaho, with two broken legs, internal injuries and much pain, *that* let S spend next week in Boise, Idaho."

S then compounds again and comes up with: "It is acceptable, *given* that let S give his mother pleasure and get ready the firm's accounts and sustain Matilda, and that S is his mother's favourite son and head accountant at accounting time and Matilda's husband with Matilda lying in Boise, Idaho (etc.), *that* let S spend next week in Boise, Idaho, and telephone his mother and his office daily."

(S, we may add, has rejected, or rated lower, a conditional with the same complex antecedent and a variant consequent, namely, "Let S remove Matilda from hospital and take her around with him to Milwaukee and to Redwood City.")

Being conscientious about practical inference, S searches (duly) for a further disturbing conditional, finds none, and applies detachment to the last conditional, arriving at: "It is acceptable that let S spend next week in Boise, telephoning his mother and his office daily."

Now if (as surely we must) we take this example as a paradigm of a certain kind of practical reasoning, it looks to me as if the proposed formulation of a PTE could be applied to it without change, apart from the deletion of the word 'alethic' and the substitution of the word 'practical'. There is the same search for a disturbing feature to upset an acceptability-conditional which thus far holds the day, the same failure to find it, and the same readiness, at that point, to apply detachment.

There are, however, two comments which need to be made which might point to features of practical acceptabilities which would threaten an attempt to represent the common modals in which I am interested as being univocal, or equally multivocal, across the board. (1) I have taken an example in which the 'subject' S (the reasoner) and the particular object to which the acceptability-conditionals refer are *one and the same*; and one would certainly need to enquire what pertains when they are different; and (2) there may well be, in practical acceptabilities, a concealed relativity to a particular individual in the idea of a set of *competing* consequents, which my formulation of PTE makes use of. For 'rival' possible consequents might have to be described as specifying members of a set of actions or states of affairs which are possible, open, or achievable; and then the questions "possible for whom?", "achievable by whom?" might be embarrassing, as compelling a relativization of *practical* modals to particular persons. Would we be talking about achievability or possibility for the reasoner, for the subject of the acceptability-conditional, or for some third party? I shall not expand on these matters at this point, since they are closely related to enquiries which I shall address in the next chapter.

Bating these anxieties, when we advert to non-weighted *ceteris paribus* acceptabilities, I also see no reason why the propounded

If   (*a*) S accepts at t an alethic (practical) acceptability-conditional C_1, the antecedent of which favours (to degree d) the consequent of C_1,

(*b*) S accepts at t the antecedent of C_1,

(*c*) after due search by S for such a (further) conditional, there is no conditional C_2 such that

(1) S accepts at t C_2, and its antecedent,

and (2) the antecedent of C_2 is an extension of the antecedent of C_1,

and (3) the consequent of C_2 is a rival (incompatible with) of the consequent of C_1,

and (4) the antecedent of C_2 favours the consequent of C_2 more than it favours the consequent of C_1:

then S may judge (accept) at t that the consequent of C_1 is acceptable (to degree d).

Note: Omit phrases in brackets for unweighted kind of acceptability.

FIG. 3. Formulation of a Principle of Total Evidence

formulation of PTE should not be applied both in the alethic and the practical dimensions, provided of course that references to weights or degrees are eliminated by deletion of the phrases which on Fig. 3 are enclosed in brackets. There is, however, sometimes detectable in this region a situation in which, when we come to apply detachment, we are in a stronger position than that which I have so far been envisaging. The phenomenon in question might perhaps arise not only with regard to weighted acceptabilities; but of this I am uncertain. It is, as I shall indicate, of some philosophical interest.

Consider a not wholly realistic example. A doctor is considering how to treat a patient whom I shall call "Pidduck". I shall phrase his reflections in terms of the expressions 'ought*', 'must*', and the colloquial 'is to' (*vice* "let it be that"). The doctor has, or has available to him, the following acceptability-conditionals, each of them derived by instantiation from a *ceteris paribus* generalization which is (we pretend) well established.

(1) "Given that Pidduck is to be relieved of cephalalgia (an ailment, a common symptom of which is headache), and that Pidduck is of blood group O, *then* Pidduck ought* to take aspirin."

(2) "Given that Pidduck is to be relieved of cephalalgia and also of gasteroplexis (an ailment, a common symptom of which is stomach cramp), and that Pidduck is of blood group O, *then* Pidduck ought* to be treated by electromixosis (the very latest thing in this region of therapy)."

(3) "Given that Pidduck is to be relieved of cephalalgia and also of gasteroplexis, and that Pidduck is of blood group O and that his blood has an abnormally high alcohol content, *then* Pidduck ought* to be given gentle massage until his condition changes."

The doctor accepts the antecedents of the first two conditionals, but *rejects* the antecedent of the third; he does not find an abnormally high alcohol content in Pidduck's blood. Not only, however, does he reject the antecedent of conditional (3), but he considers that he has ample grounds for rejecting the antecedent of *any* conditional which extends the antecedent of (2); he regards Pidduck's condition as a perfectly normal case of cephalalgia combined with gasteroplexis; though there are (perhaps indefinitely many) *good* ceteris paribus *generalizations* with antecedents extending the antecedent of the generalization from which conditional (2) is derived, he is confident that none of them applies to *Pidduck*. In such a situation, I suggest, the doctor is entitled to treat (in a non-medical sense) Pidduck's case *as if* it fell under a *full*-acceptability generalization (one which is not defeasible), which would be expressed by changing, in the generalization of (2), the word 'ought*' to the word 'must*'. He can then at once apply detachment, and decide (think) that Pidduck must* be given electromixosis.

The licence, in circumstances comparable with these, to shift from 'ought*' to 'must*' is relevant to a celebrated complaint about Kant's ethical theory. Expressed in my terms, I think that Kant believed that imperfect or 'meritorious' obligations, such as the obligation to develop one's talents or to help others, could be allowed to fall under generalizations ascribing one or other form of defeasible practical acceptability; we could (in his terms) allow here conflicting *grounds* of obligation, though not conflicting *obligations*. But with respect to *perfect* or *strict* obligations, like obligations to tell the truth or to keep promises, this treatment is not available; such obligations have to be thought of as matters of practical *law*, as falling (that is) under generalizations which invoke full (unqualified) practical acceptability. I suspect that he took this position partly from certain theoretical considerations and partly because he felt that, if he allowed the possibility of exceptions in such cases, allowed the 'must' to become an 'ought' (in the vernacular sense), he would be failing to capture the *stringency* which he felt to attach to particular cases of perfect obligation. His 'hard line' in this matter has brought down on his head a modicum of ridicule, in respect of his well-known contention that one should tell the truth even to a would-be murderer searching for his intended victim.

It seems to me that one could honour Kant's non-theoretical motivation, and at the same time save him from ridicule, by an application of the licence which I have sketched. I have not yet attempted to characterize the form of 'moral' acceptabilities, but let us suppose that, in the first instance, they differ from the practical acceptabilities which I have distinguished in that the generalizations associated with them *omit*, from their *antecedents*, any 'volitive' sub-clause; they are of the form Acc ($\vdash$ Fx; ! Gx). Now it would be quite open to us to maintain that even the generalizations connected with 'perfect obligation' are of the *ceteris paribus* variety, and so to be expressed in terms of 'ought*'; but that, at the same time, it very often happens that, with respect to a particular case, we know that none of the sometimes defeating features applies; and so that, with respect to such cases, one is authorized to shift from 'ought*' to 'must*'. This seems to me to be not only a position which would both preserve Kant's intuition and save him from ridicule, but to be also a position of considerable plausibility.

Embedding of Mode-Markers and Satisfactoriness

I should like to begin the final section of this chapter with a reminder of, and a slight enlargement upon, a fragment of the later part of the first chapter. Speaking from a 'genitorial' point of view,[2] I would regard reasoning as a faculty for enlarging our acceptances by the application of *forms* of transition, from a set of acceptances to a further acceptance, which are such as to ensure the transmission of *value* from premises to conclusion, should such value attach to the premises. By 'value' I mean some property which is of value (of a certain *kind* of value, no doubt). Truth is one such property, but it may not be the only one; and we have now reached a point

---

[2] For a discussion of the "genitorial point of view", see Paul Grice, "Reply to Richards", in Richard Grandy and Richard Warner (eds.), *Philosophical Grounds of Rationality: Intentions, Categories, Ends* (Oxford: Oxford University Press, 1986).

at which we can identify another, namely, *practical* value (good-ness). So each of these should be thought of as special cases of a more general notion of *satisfactoriness*.

Let us work out a little more fully, though abstractly, how such a treatment might be constructed.

Stage 1. We have sentence-radicals which qualify for 'radical truth' or 'radical falsity'; some of those which so qualify, also qualify for 'radical goodness' or 'radical badness'.

Stage 2. We have judicative sentences ('⊢'-sentences) which are assigned truth (or falsity) just in case their radicals qualify for radical truth (or radical falsity); and we have volitive sentences ('!' sentences) which are assigned practical value (or disvalue) just in case their radicals qualify for radical goodness (or badness). Since the sentential forms will indicate which kind of value is involved, we can use the *generic* term 'satisfactory'.

Stage 3. We import into the object language the phrases 'It is true that' and 'It is good that'; 'It is true that ⊢ p' is to be satis-factory qua true just in case '⊢ p' is satisfactory qua true; and 'it is good that ! p' is to be satisfactory qua *true* just in case '! p' is satisfactory qua having *practical value*.

At *Stage 4* we introduce 'it is acceptable that' (with the syn-tactical provisions which I have been using); on the practical side, 'It is acceptable that ! p' will be true just in case 'it is good that ! p' is true.

We could now, if we wished, introduce generalized versions of some standard binary connectives; using 'φ' and 'ψ' to represent sentences (in either mode), we could stipulate that ⌜φ & ψ⌝ is satisfactory just in case ⌜φ⌝ is satisfactory and ⌜ψ⌝ is satisfactory, ⌜φ or ψ⌝ is satisfactory just in case one of the pair, ⌜φ and ψ⌝, is satisfactory, and ⌜φ → ψ⌝ is satisfactory just in case either ⌜φ⌝ is unsatisfactory or ⌜ψ⌝ is satisfactory. There are, however, a num-ber of points to be made.

(1) It is not fully clear to me just how strong the motivation would be for introducing such connectives, nor whether, if they are introduced, restrictions should not be imposed. The problematic examples will be, of course, the *mixed* ones (those in which one clause is judicative and the other volitive). It seems natural to look

for guidance from ordinary speech. "The beast is filthy and don't (I shan't) touch it" seems all right, but "Don't touch the beast and it is filthy" seems dubious, and "Touch the beast and it will bite you", while idiomatic, is not a conjunction, nor a genuine invitation to touch the beast. And "Either he is taking a bath or leave the bathroom door open" is perhaps intelligible, but "Leave the bathroom door open or he is taking a bath" seems considerably less so.

(2) It is perhaps worth noting that, in unmixed cases, satisfactoriness would be specifiable either as satisfactoriness qua truth or as satisfactoriness qua practical value; but for *mixed* cases no such specification would be available unless we make a special stipulation (for example, that the volitive mode is to be dominant).

(3) The real crunch comes, however, with negation (which I have been carefully ignoring). 'Not ⊦ p' might perhaps be treated as equivalent to '⊦ not-p', but what about 'Not ! p'? What do we say in cases like, perhaps, "Let it be that I now put my hand on my head" or "Let it be that my bicycle faces north", in which (at least on occasion) it seems to be that neither '! A' nor '! ~ A' is either satisfactory or unsatisfactory? What value do we assign to '~ ! A' and to '~ ! ~ A'? Do we proscribe the forms altogether (for *all* cases)? But that would seem to be a pity, since '~ ! ~ A' seems to be quite promising as a representation for 'you may (permissive) do A'; that is, I signify my refusal to prohibit your doing A. Do we disallow embedding of these forms? But that (again if we use them to represent 'may') seems too restrictive. Again, if '! A' is neither satisfactory nor unsatisfactory, do we assign a *third* 'value' to '! A' ('practically neuter'), or do we say that we have a 'practical value gap'? These and other such problems would require careful consideration; but I cannot see that they would prove insoluble, any more than analogous problems connected with presupposition are insoluble; in the latter case the difficulty is not so much to find a solution as to select the *best* solution from those which present themselves.

4

Practical and Alethic Reasons: Part II

Inferential Relations between Practical and Alethic Acceptabilities

I have been, so far, in the early stages of an attempt to estimate the prospects of what I shall now rename as an "*Equi*vocality Thesis" with respect to certain common modals (that is, a thesis, or set of theses, with respect to particular common modals, which claims that they are univocal across the practical/alethic divide, or if they are multivocal, then their multivocality appears equally on each side of the barrier). My strategy has been to put up as good an initial case as I could in favour of representing the use of certain modals on different sides of the barrier as explicable in terms of a single set of acceptability modals, which are to be semantically barrier-indifferent; the differences between alethic and practical acceptabilities being attributed to the semantic differences between judicative and volitive mode-markers ('⊢' and '!'), together with structural differences, such as the appearance on the practical side of "two-slot" antecedents, with 'mixed' mode-markers, in acceptability conditionals, which might reasonably themselves be attributed to differences between '⊢' and '!'. I have so far considered only volitive acceptabilities which might be thought of as more or less analogous to Kant's Technical Imperatives; and I have not yet raised any question about the inferential relations which might obtain across the barrier, in particular about the possibility that volitive acceptabilities (or some of them) might be equivalent to, or inferable from, certain alethic acceptabilities. It is time to attend to these lacunae, starting with the second. The existence of such cross-barrier inferabilities would be of interest in more than one way. (1) It would be of interest in itself, as providing some interesting general logical facts; (2) anyone who regarded practical acceptabilities as philosophically problematic, but did not feel the same way about alethic acceptabilities, might be reassured in so far as he could think of practical acceptabilities as derivable from alethic acceptabilities; (3) someone who did not regard either variety of acceptability as *specially* problematic, might well (and no doubt *should*) regard *both* as in need of philosophical justification, and it would be a step towards such justification to show that, provided certain alethic acceptabilities are justifiable, certain practical acceptabilities are also justifiable; (4) the display of such cross-barrier relations might itself be relevant to the prospects of the "*Equi*vocality Thesis".

I shall begin the substantial discussion of this topic by taking a common modal which I have not so far associated with any of the sub-varieties of acceptability, namely, the modal "should". In a certain sense, this is a slight cheat, since my purpose in so doing is to cover up some of the intricacies of detail which would complicate matters if I were to proceed with direct reference of modals already invoked; but as I intend shortly to lay bare some of that detail, perhaps my procedure might be regarded as an expository device, and so as only a *temporary* cheat.

Let us take as our example the following acceptability sentence: "To preserve a youthful complexion, if one has a relatively insensitive skin, one should smear one's face with peanut butter before retiring at night." This fascinating recipe can be thought of as being, in my scheme of representation, expressible as "It should be, given that let one preserve a youthful complexion and that one has a relatively insensitive skin, that let one smear one's face with peanut butter before retiring", or in an abbreviated general symbolism "Should (! E, ⊢ F; ! G)". Now there is at least some initial plausibility in the idea that this practical acceptability statement is satisfactory (qua true) just in case the following alethic acceptability statement is also acceptable (qua true): "It should be, given that it is the case that one smears one's skin with peanut butter before retiring and that it is the case that one has a relatively insensitive skin, that it is the case that one preserves a youthful complexion." More generally, there is some plausibility to the idea that an exemplar of the form 'Should (! E, ⊢ F; ! G)' is true just in case a corresponding examplar of the form 'Should (⊢ F, ⊢ G; ⊢ E)' is true.

Before proceeding further, I will attempt to deal briefly with a possible objection which might be raised at this point. I can imagine an ardent descriptivist, who *first* complains, in the face of someone who wishes to allow a legitimate autonomous status to practical acceptability generalizations, that truth-conditions for such generalizations are not available, and perhaps are in principle not available; so such generalizations are not to be taken seriously. We then point out to him that, at least for a class of such cases, truth-conditions are available, and that they are to be found in related alethic generalizations, a kind of generalization he accepts. He *then* complains that, if finding truth-conditions involves representing the practical acceptability generalizations as being true just in case related alethic generalizations are true, then practical acceptability generalizations are simply *reducible* to alethic generalizations, and so are not to be taken seriously for another reason, namely, that they are simply *transformations* of alethic generalizations, and we could perfectly well get on without them. Maybe some of you have heard some ardent descriptivists arguing in a style not so very different from this. Now a deep reply to such an objection would involve (I think) a display of the need for a system of reasoning in which the value to be transmitted by acceptable inference is not truth but practical value, together with a demonstration of the role of practical acceptability generalizations in such a system. I suspect that such a reply could be constructed, but I do not have it at my fingertips (or tongue-tip), so I shall not try to produce it. An interim reply, however, might take the following form: even though it may be true (which is by no means certain) that certain practical acceptability generalizations have the same truth-conditions as certain corresponding alethic generalizations, it is not to be supposed that the former generalizations are simply reducible to the latter (in some disrespectful sense of 'reducible'). For though both kinds of generalization are *defeasible*, they are not defeasible in the same way; more exactly, what is a defeating condition for a given practical generalization is not a defeating condition for its alethic counterpart. A generalization of the form 'should (! E, ⊢ F; ! G)' may have, as a defeating condition, 'E*'; that is to say, consistently with the truth of this generalization, it may be true that 'should (! E & ! E*, ⊢ F; ! G*)' where 'G*' is inconsistent with 'G'. But since, in the alethic counterpart generalization 'should (⊢ F, ⊢ G; ⊢ E)', 'E' does *not* occur in the antecedent, 'E*' *cannot* be a defeating condition for *this* generalization. And, since liability to defeat by a certain range of defeating conditions is essential to the role which acceptability generalizations play in reasoning, this difference between a practical generalization and its alethic counterpart is sufficient to eliminate the reducibility of the former to the latter.

To return to the main theme of this section. If, without further ado, we were to accept at this point the suggestion that 'should (! E, ⊢ F; ! G)' is true just in case 'should (⊢ F, ⊢ G; ⊢ E)' is true, we should be accepting it simply on the basis of intuition (including, of course, linguistic or logical intuition under the head of 'intuition'). If the suggestion is correct then we should attain, at the same time, a stronger assurance that it is correct and a better theoretical understanding of the alethic and practical acceptability, if we could show *why* it is correct by deriving it from some general principle(s). Kant, in fact, for reasons not unlike these, sought to show the validity of a different but fairly closely related Technical Imperative by just such a method. The form which he selects is one which, in my terms, would be represented by "It is fully acceptable, given let it be that B, that let it be that A" or "It is necessary, given let it be that B, that let it be that A". Applying this to the one fully stated technical imperative given in *Grundlegung*, we get "It is necessary, given let it be that one bisect a line on an unerring principle, that let it be that I draw from its extremities two intersecting arcs". Call this statement, (∝). Though he does not express himself very clearly, I am certain that his claim is that this imperative is validated in virtue of the fact that it is, analytically, a consequence of an indicative statement which is true and, in the present context, unproblematic, namely, the statement vouched for by geometry, that if one bisects a line on an unerring principle, then one does so *only* as a result of having drawn from its extremities two intersecting arcs. Call this statement, (β). His argument *seems* to be expressible as follows.

(1) It is analytic that he who wills the end (so far as reason decides his conduct), wills the indispensable means thereto.

So (2) it is analytic that (so far as one is rational) *if* one wills that A, and judges that if A, then A as a result of B, *then* one wills that B.

So (3) it is analytic that (so far as one is rational) *if* one judges that if A, then A as a result of B, *then* if one wills that A then one wills that B.

So (4) it is analytic that, *if* it is true that if A, then A as a result of B, *then* if let it be that A, then it must be that let it be that B.

From which, by substitution, we derive (5): it is analytic that if β then α.

Now it seems to me to be meritorious, on Kant's part, *first* that he saw a need to justify hypothetical imperatives of this sort, which it is only too easy to take for granted, and *second* that he invoked the principle that "he who wills the end, wills the means"; intuitively, this invocation seems right. Unfortunately, however, the step from (3) to (4) seems open to dispute on two different counts. (1) It looks as if an unwarranted 'must' has appeared in the consequent of the conditional which is claimed, in (4), as analytic; the most that, to all appearances, could be claimed as being true of the antecedent is that 'if let it be that A then let it be that B'. (2) (Perhaps more serious.) It is by no means clear by what right the psychological verbs 'judge' and 'will', which appear in (3), are omitted in (4); how does an (alleged) analytic connection between (i) *judging* that if A, A as a result of B and (ii) its being the case that if one *wills* that A then one wills that B yield an analytic connection between (i) *it's being the case* that if A, A as a result of B and (ii) the 'proposition' that if let it be that A then let it be that B? Can the presence in (3) of the phrase "in so far as one is rational" legitimize this step?

I do not know what remedy to propose for the first of these two difficulties; but I will attempt a reconstruction of Kant's line of argument which *might* provide relief from the second. It might, indeed, even be an expansion of Kant's actual thinking; but whether or not this is so, I am a very long way from being confident in its adequacy.

(1) Let us suppose it to be a *fundamental* psychological law that, *ceteris paribus*, for any creature x (of a sufficiently developed kind), no matter what A and B are, *if* x wills A and judges that if A, A only as a result of B, *then* x wills B. This I take to be a proper representation of "he who wills the end, wills the indispensable means"; and in calling it a *fundamental* law I mean that it is the

law, or one of the laws, from which 'willing' and 'judging' derive their sense as names of concepts which explain behaviour. So, I assume, to reject it would be to *deprive* these words of their sense. If x is a *rational* creature, since in this case his attitudes of acceptance are at least to some degree under his control (volitive or judicative assent can be *withheld* or *refused*), this law will hold for him only if the following is true:

(2) x wills (it is x's will) that (for any A, B) if x wills that A and judges that if A, A only as a result of B, then x is to will that B.

In so far as x proceeds rationally, x should will as specified in (2) only if x judges that if it is satisfactory to will that A and also satisfactory to judge that if A, A only as a result of B, then it is satisfactory to will that B; otherwise, in willing as specified in (2), he will be willing to run the risk of passing from satisfactory attitudes to unsatisfactory ones. So, given that x wills as specified in (2):

(3) x *should* (qua rational) judge that (for any A, B) *if* it is satisfactory to will that A and also satisfactory to judge that if A, A only as a result of B, *then* it is satisfactory to will that B.

Since the satisfactoriness of attitudes of acceptance resolves itself into the satisfactoriness (in the sense distinguished in the previous chapter) of the *contents* of those attitudes (marked by the appropriate mode-markers), if x judges as specified in (3) then:

(4) x *should* (qua rational) judge that (for any A, B) *if* it is satisfactory that ! A and also satisfactory that if it is the case that A, A only as a result of B, *then* it is satisfactory that ! B.

And, if x judges as in (4), then (because (A & B → C) yields A → (B → C)):

(5) x *should* judge that (for any A, B) *if* it is satisfactory that if A, A only because B, then it is satisfactory that, if let it be that A, then let it be that B.

But if x judges that satisfactoriness is, for any A, B, transmitted in this particular way, then:

(6) x *should* judge that (for any A, B) if A, A only because B, *yields* if let it be that A, then let it be that B.

But if *any rational* being should (qua rational) *judge* that (for any A, B) the first 'propositional' form yields the second, then the first propositional form *does* yield the second; so:

(7) (For any A, B) if A, A only because B *yields* if let it be that A, then let it be that B.

(A special apology for the particularly violent disregard of 'use and mention'; my usual reason is offered.)

Fig. 4 summarizes the steps of the argument.

I. *Kant's steps*

α = It is necessary, given let it be that one bisect a line on an unerring principle, that let it be that I draw from its extremities two intersecting arcs.

β = If one bisects a line on an unerring principle, then one does so only as a result of having drawn from its extremities two intersecting arcs.

(1) It is analytic that (so far as he is rational) he who wills the end wills the means.

(2) It is analytic that (so far as one is rational) *if* one wills that A, and judges that if A, then A only as a result of B, *then* one wills that B.

(3) It is analytic that (so far as one is rational) *if* one judges that if A, A as a result of B, *then* if one wills that A one wills that B.

(4) It is analytic that *if*, if A, then A as a result of B, *then*, if let it be that A, then it must be that let it be that B.

(5) It is analytic that if β, then α.

II. *Reconstruction steps*

(1) Fundamental law that (*ceteris paribus*) for any creature x (for any A, B), *if* x wills A and judges that if A, then A as a result of B; *then* x wills B.

(2) x wills that (for any A, B) *if* x wills A and judges that if A, A as a result of B, then x is to will that B.

(3) x *should* (qua rational) judge that (for any A, B) *if* it is satisfactory to will that A and also satisfactory to judge that if A, A only as a result of B, *then* it is satisfactory to will that B.

(4) x *should* (qua rational) judge that (for any A, B) *if* it is satisfactory that ! A and also satisfactory that if ⊢ A, then ⊢ A only as a result of B, *then* it is satisfactory that ! B.

(5) x *should* (q.r.) judge that (for any A, B) *if* it is satisfactory that if ⊢ A, ⊢ A only because B, *then* it is satisfactory that, if let it be that A, then let it be that B.

(6) x *should* (q.r.) judge that (for any A, B) if A, A only because B, *yields* if let it be that A, then let it be that B.

(7) (For any A, B) if A, A only because B *yields* if let it be that A, then let it be that B.

FIG. 4. Validation of technical acceptabilities

Prudential Acceptability

It will be convenient to initiate the discussion of this topic by again referring to Kant. Kant thought that there is a special sub-class of Hypothetical Imperatives (which he called "counsels of prudence") which were like his class of Technical Imperatives, except in that the end *specified* in a full statement of the imperative is the special end of Happiness (one's happiness). To translate into my terminology, this seems to amount to the thesis that there is a special subclass of, for example, singular practical acceptability conditionals which exemplifies the structure "it is acceptable, given that let *a* (an individual) be happy, that let *a* be (do) G"; an additional indicative sub-antecedent ("that it is the case that *a* is F") might be sometimes needed, and could be added without difficulty. There would, presumably, be a corresponding special subclass of acceptability generalizations. The main characteristics which Kant would attribute to such prudential acceptability conditionals would, I think, be the following.

(1) The foundation for such conditionals is exactly the same as that for technical imperatives; they would be treated as being, in principle, analytically consequences of indicative statements to the effect that so-and-so is a (the) means to such-and-such. The relation between my doing philosophy now and my being happy would be a causal relation not significantly different from the relation between my taking an aspirin and my being relieved of my headache.

(2) However, though the relation would be the same, the question whether *in fact* my doing philosophy now will promote my happiness is insoluble; to solve it, I should have to be omniscient, since I should have to determine that my doing philosophy now would lead to "a maximum of welfare in my present and all future circumstances".

(3) The special end (happiness) of specific prudential acceptability conditionals is one which we know that, as a matter of "natural necessity", every human being has; so, unlike technical imperatives, their applicability to himself cannot be disclaimed by any human being.

(4) Before we bring in the demands of morality (which will pre-scribe concern for our own happiness as a *derivative* duty), the only positive evaluation of a desire for one's happiness is an alethic evalu-ation; one *ought* to, or *must*, desire one's own happiness only in the sense that, whoever one may be, it is acceptable that *it is the case* that one desire one's own happiness; the 'ought' or 'must' is non-practical. (This position seems to me akin to a Humean appeal to '*natural dispositions*', in place of *justification*.)

I would wish to disagree with Kant in two, or possibly three, ways.

(1) Kant, I think, did not devote a great deal of thought to the nature of happiness, no doubt because he regarded it as being of little importance to the philosophical foundations of morality. So it is not clear whether he regarded happiness as a *distinct* end from the variety of ends which one might pursue with a view to happiness, rather than as a complex end which includes (in some sense of 'include') some of such ends. If he did regard it as a dis-tinct end, then I think he was wrong.

(2) I think he was certainly wrong in thinking of something's being conducive to happiness as being on all fours with, say, some-thing's being conducive to the relief of a headache; as, perhaps, a matter (in both cases) of causal relationship.

(3) I would *like* to think him wrong in thinking that (morality apart) there is no *practical* interpretation of 'ought' in which one ought to pursue (desire, aim at) one's own happiness.

We have, then, three not unconnected questions which demand some attention.

(A) What is the *nature* of happiness?
(B) In what sense (if any) (and why) *should* I desire, or aim at, my own happiness?
(C) What is the nature of the connection between things which are conducive to happiness and happiness? (What, specifically, is implied by 'conducive'?)

Though it is fiendishly difficult, I shall take up question (C) first. I trust that I will be forgiven if I do not present a full and coherent answer.

Let us take a brief look at Aristotle. Aristotle was, I think, more sophisticated in this area.

(1) Though it is by no means beyond dispute, I am disposed to think that he did regard Happiness (*eudaemonia*) as a complex end 'containing' (in some sense) the ends which are constitutive of happiness; to use the jargon of recent commentators, I suspect he regarded it as an 'inclusive' and not a 'dominant' end.

(2) He certainly thought that one should (practical 'should') aim at one's own happiness.

(3) (The matter directly relevant to my present purpose.) I strongly suspect that he did not think that the relationship between, say, my doing philosophy and my happiness was a straightforward causal relationship. The passage which I have in mind is *Nicomachean Ethics* VI. 12, 13, where he distinguishes between wisdom ("practical wisdom") and cleverness (or, one might say, resourcefulness). He there makes the following statements: (*a*) that wisdom is not the same as cleverness, though *like* it, (*b*) that wisdom does not exist *without* cleverness, (*c*) that wisdom is always laudable (to be wise one must be virtuous), but cleverness is not always laudable, for example, in rogues, (*d*) that the relation between wisdom and cleverness is analogous to the relation between 'natural' virtue and virtue proper (he says this in the same place as he says (*a*)). Faced with these not exactly voluminous remarks, some commentators have been led (not I think without reluctance) to interpret Aristotle as holding that the *only* difference between wisdom and cleverness is that the former does, and the latter does not, require the presence of virtue; to be wise is simply to be clever in good causes. Apart from the fact that additional difficulties are generated thereby, with respect to the interpretation of *Nicomachean Ethics* VI, to attribute this view to Aristotle does not seem to indicate a very high respect for *his* wisdom, particularly as the text does not seem to *demand* such an interpretation.

Following an idea once given me, long ago, by Austin, I would prefer to think of Aristotle as distinguishing between the characteristic manifestation of wisdom, namely, the ability to determine *what* one should do (*what* should be done), and the characteristic manifestation of cleverness, which is the ability to determine *how* to do what it is that should be done. On this interpretation cleverness would plainly be in a certain sense subordinate to wisdom, since opportunity for cleverness (and associated qualities) will only

arise after there has been some determination of what it is that is
to be done. It may also be helpful (suggestive) to think of wisdom
as being (or being assimilable to) *administrative* ability, with cleverness being comparable with *executive* ability. I would also like to
connect cleverness, initially, with the ability to recognize (devise)
technical acceptabilities (though its scope might be larger than this),
while wisdom is shown primarily in other directions. On such
assumptions, expansion of the still obscure Aristotelian distinction
is plainly a way of pursuing question (C), or questions closely
related to it; for we will be asking what other kinds of acceptabilities
(beyond 'technical' acceptabilities) we need in order to engage (or
engage effectively) in practical reasoning. I fear my contribution
here will be sketchy and not very systematic.

We might start by exploring a little further the 'administrative/
executive' distinction, a distinction which, I must admit, is extremely
hazy and also not at all hard and fast (lines might be drawn, in
different cases, in quite different places). A boss tells his secretary
that he will be travelling on business to such-and-such places, next
week, and asks her to arrange travel and accommodation for him.
I suspect that there is nothing peculiar about that. But suppose,
instead of giving her those instructions, he had said to her that he
wanted to travel on business somewhere or other, next week, and
asked her to arrange destinations, matters to be negotiated, firms
to negotiate with, and brief him about what to say to those whom
he would visit. That would be a little more unusual, and the secretary *might* reply angrily, "I am paid to be your secretary, not to run
your business for you, let alone run *you*." What (philosophically)
differentiates the two cases?

Let us call a desire or intention D which a man has at t "terminal for him at t" if there is no desire or intention which he has
at t, which is more specific than D; if, for example, a man wanted
at t a car, but it was also true of him that he wanted a Mercedes,
then his desire for a car would not be terminal. Now I think we can
(roughly) distinguish (at least) three ways in which a terminal desire
may be non-specific.

(1) D may be *finitely* non-specific; for example, a man may want
a large, fierce dog (to guard his house) and not care at all what
kind of large, fierce dog he acquired; any kind will do (at least within

some normal range). Furthermore, he does not envisage his attitude, that any kind will do, being changed when action-time comes; he will of course get some particular kind of dog, but what kind will simply depend on such things as availability.

(2) D may be *indeterminately* non-specific: that is to say the desirer may recognize, and intend, that before he acts the desire or intention D should be made *more* specific than it is; he has decided, say, that he wants a large, fierce dog, but has not *yet* decided what kind he wants. It seems to me that an *indeterminately* non-specific desire or intention differs from a finitely non-specific desire in a way which is relevant to the application of the concept of 'means-taking'. If the man with the finitely non-specific desire for a large, fierce dog decides on a mastiff, that would be (or at least could be) a case of choosing a mastiff as a means to having a large, fierce dog, but not something of which getting a large, fierce dog would be an *effect*. But, if the man with the *indeterminate* desire for a large, fierce dog decides that he wants a mastiff (as a further determination of that indeterminate desire), that is not a case of means-picking at all.

(3) There is a further kind of non-specificity which I mention only with a view to completeness: a desire D may be *vaguely*, or indefinitely, non-specific; a man may have decided that he wants a large, fierce dog, but it may not be very well defined what could *count* as a large, fierce dog; a mastiff would count, and a Pekinese would not, but what about a red setter? In such cases the desire or intention needs to be *interpreted*, but not to be further specified.

With regard to the first two kinds of non-specificity, there are some remarks to be made.

(1) We do not usually (if we are sensible) make our desires more determinate than the occasion demands; if getting a dog is not a present prospect, a man who decides *exactly* what kind of dog he would like is engaging in fantasy.

(2) The final stage of determination may be left to the occasion of action; if I want to buy some fancy curtains, I may leave the full determination of the kind until I see them in the store.

(3) Circumstances may change the status of a desire; a man may have a *finitely* non-specific desire for a dog until he talks to

his wife, who changes things for him (making his desire *indeterminately* non-specific).

(4) Indeterminately non-specific desires may of course be founded (and well founded) on reasons, and so may be not merely desires one *does* have but also desires which one *should* have.

We may now return to the boss and his secretary. It seems to me that what the 'normally' behaved boss does (assuming that he has a very new and inexperienced secretary) is to reach a *finitely* non-specific desire or intention (or a set of such), communicate these to his secretary, and leave to her the implementation of this (these) intention(s); he presumes that nothing which she will do, and no problem which she will encounter, will disturb his intention (for, within reasonable limits, he does not *care* what she does), even though her execution of her tasks may well involve considerable skill and diplomacy (*deinotes*). If she is more senior, then he may well not himself reach a *finitely*, but only an *indeterminately*, non-specific intention, leaving it to her to complete the determination and trusting her to do so more or less as he would himself. If she reaches a position in which she is empowered to make determinate his intentions not as she thinks *he* would think best, but as *she* thinks best, then I would say that she has ceased to be a secretary and has become an administrative assistant.

This might be a convenient place to refer briefly to a distinction which is of some importance in practical thinking which is not just a matter of finding a means, of one sort or another, to an already fixed goal, and which is fairly closely related to the process of *determination* which I have been describing. This is the distinction between *non-propositional* ends, like power, wealth, skill at chess, gardening; and *propositional* or *objective* ends, like to get the Dean to agree with my proposal, or that my uncle should go to jail for his peculations of the family money. Non-propositional ends are in my view *universals*, the kind of items to be named by mass-terms or abstract nouns. I should like to regard their non-propositional appearance as *genuine*; I would like them to be not only things which we can be said to pursue, but also things which we can be said to *care about*; and I would not want to reduce 'caring about' to 'caring that', though of course there is an intimate connection between these kinds of caring. I would like to make the following points.

(1) Non-propositional ends enter into the most primitive kinds of psychological explanation; the behaviour of lower animals is to be explained in terms of their wanting *food*, not of their wanting (say) to eat an apple.

(2) Non-propositional ends are characteristically variable in degree, and the degrees are valuationally ordered; for one who wants wealth, a greater degree of wealth is (normally) preferable to a lesser degree.

(3) They are the type, I think, to which ultimate ends which are constitutive of happiness belong; and not without reason, since their non-propositional, and often non-temporal, character renders them fit members of an enduring system which is designed to guide conduct in particular cases.

(4) The process of *determination* applies to them, indeed, starts with them; desire for power is (say) rendered more determinate as desire for political power; and objectives (to get the position of Prime Minister) may be reached by determination applied to non-propositional ends.

(5) Though it is clear to me that the distinction exists, and that a number of particular items can be placed on one side or another of the barrier, there is a host of uncertain examples, and the distinction is not easy to *apply*.

Let us now look at things from her (the secretary's) angle. *First*, many (indeed most) of the things she does, though perhaps cases of means-finding, will not be cases of finding means of the kind which philosophers usually focus on, namely, causal means. She gets him an air-ticket, which *enables*, but does not *cause*, him to travel to Kalamazoo, Michigan; she arranges by telephone for him to stay at the Hotel Goosepimple; his being booked in there is not an *effect* but an intended *outcome* of her conversation on the telephone; and his being booked in at *that* hotel is not a *cause* of his being booked at a hotel, but a *way* in which that situation or circumstance is realized. *Second*, if during her operations she discovers that there is an epidemic of yellow fever at Kalamazoo, she does not (unless she wishes to be fired) go blindly ahead and book him in; she consults him, because something has now happened which will (if he knows of it) disturb his finitely non-specific intention; indeed *may* confront the boss with a *plurality* of conflicting (or apparently conflicting) ends or desiderata; a situation which is next in line for consideration. Before turning to it, however, I think I should remark that the kind of features which have shown up in this interpersonal transaction are also characteristic of solitary deliberation, when the deliberator executes his own decisions.

We are now, we suppose, at a stage at which the secretary has come back to the boss to announce that if she executes the task given her (implements the decision about what to do which he has reached), there is such-and-such a snag; that is, the decision can be implemented only at the cost of a consequence which will (or which she suspects may) dispromote some further end which he wants to promote, or promote some "counter-end" which he wants to dispromote.

(1) We may remark that this kind of problem is not something which only arises *after* a finitely non-specific intention has been formed; exactly parallel problems are frequently, though not invariably, encountered on the way towards a finitely non-specific intention or desire. This prompts a further comment on Aristotle's remark that, though wisdom is not identical with cleverness, wisdom does not exist without cleverness. This dictum covers two distinct truths; *first*, that if a man were good at deciding what to do, but *terrible* at executing it (he makes a hash of working out train times, he is tactless with customs officials, he irritates hotel clerks into non-cooperation), one might hesitate to confer upon him the title 'wise'; at least a modicum of cleverness is required. *Second*, and more interestingly, cleverness is liable to be manifested at all stages of deliberation; every time a snag arises in connection with a tentative determination of one's will, provided that the snag is not blatantly obvious, *some* degree of cleverness is manifested in seeing that, if one does such-and-such (as one contemplates doing), *then* there will be the undesirable result that so-and-so.

(2) The boss may now have to determine how 'deep' the snag is, how radically his plan will have to be altered to surmount it. To lay things out a bit, the boss *might* (in some sense of 'might'), in his deliberation, have formed successively a series of indeterminately non-specific intentions ($I_i, I_{ii}, I_{iii}, \ldots I_n$), where each

member is a more specific *determination* of its predecessor, and I_n represents the final decision which he imparted to the secretary. He now (the idea is) goes back to this sequence to find the *most general* (*least* specific) member which is such that if he has *that* intention, then he is saddled with the unwanted consequences. He then knows where modification is required. Of course, in practice he may *very well* not have constructed such a convenient sequence; if he has not, then he has partially to construct one on receipt of the bad news from the secretary, to construct one (that is) which is just sufficiently well filled in to enable him to be confident that a particular element in it is the most generic intention of those he has, which generates the undesirable consequence.

Having now decided which desire or intention to remove, how does he decide what to put in its place? How, in effect, does he 'compound' his surviving end or ends with the new desideratum, the attainment of the end (or the avoidance of the counter-end) which has been brought to light by the snag? Now I have to confess that in connection with this kind of problem, I used to entertain a certain kind of picture. Let us label (for simplicity) initially just two ends E^1 and E^2, with degrees of "objective desirability" d_1 and d_2. For any action a_1 which might realize E^1, or E^2, there will be a certain probability p_1 that it will realize E^1, a certain probability p_2 that it will realize E^2, and a probability p_{12} (a function of p_1 and p_2) that it will realize both. If E^1 and E^2 are inconsistent (again, for simplicity, let us suppose they are) p_{12} will be zero. We can now, in principle, characterize the desirability of the action a_1, relative to each end (E^1 and E^2), and to each combination of ends (here just E^1 and E^2), as a function of the desirability of the end and the probability that the action a_1 will realize that end, or combination of ends. If we envisage a range of possible actions, which includes a_1 together with other actions, we can imagine that each such action has a certain degree of desirability relative to each end (E^1 and (or) E^2) and to their combination. If we suppose that, for each possible action, these desirabilities can be compounded (perhaps added), then we can suppose that one particular possible action scored higher (in action-desirability relative to these ends) than any alternative possible action; and that this is the action which wins out; that is, is the action which *is*, or at least *should*, be performed. (The computation would in fact be more complex than I have described, once account is taken of the fact that the ends involved are often not *definite* (*determinate*) states of affairs (like becoming President), but are *variable* in respect of the degree to which they might be realized (if one's end is to make a profit from a deal, that profit might be of a varying magnitude); so one would have to consider not merely the likelihood of a particular action's realizing the end of making a profit, but also the likelihood of its realizing that end *to this or that degree*; and this would considerably complicate the computational problem.)

No doubt most readers are far too sensible ever to have entertained any picture even remotely resembling the "Crazy-Bayesy" one I have just described. I was not, of course, so foolish as to suppose that such a picture represents the manner in which anybody *actually* decides what to do, though I did (at one point) consider the possibility that it might *mirror*, or *reflect*, a process actually taking place in the physiological underpinnings of psychological states (desires and beliefs), a process in the 'animal spirits', so to speak. I rather thought that it might represent an *ideal*, a procedure which is certainly *unrealized* in fact, and quite possibly one which is *in principle unrealizable* in fact, but still something to which the procedures we actually use might be thought of as *approximations*, something for which they are *substitutes*; with the additional thought that the *closer* the approximation the better the procedure. The inspirational source of such pictures as this seems to me to be the very pervasive conception of a mechanical model for the operations of the soul; desires are like *forces* to which we are subject; and their influence on us, in combination, is like the vectoring of forces. I am not at all sure that I regard this as a *good* model; the strength of its appeal may depend considerably on the fact that *some* model is needed, and that, if this one is not chosen, it is not clear what alternative model is available.

If we are not to make use of any variant of my one-time picture, how are we to give a general representation of the treatment of conflicting or competing ends? It seems to me that, for example, the accountant with the injured wife in Boise might, in the first instance, try to keep everything, to fulfil all relevant ends; he might think of telephoning Redwood City to see if his firm could postpone for a week the preparation of their accounts. If this is ineffective, then he would operate on some system of *priorities*. Looking after his wife plainly takes precedence over attention to his firm's accounting, and over visiting his mother. But having settled on measures which provide adequately for his wife's needs, he then makes whatever adjustments he can to provide for the ends which have lost the day. What he does *not* do, as a rule, is to compromise; even with regard to his previous decision involving the conflict between the claims of his firm and his mother, substantially he adopted a plan which would satisfy the claims of the firm, incorporating therein a weekend with mother as a way of doing what he could for her, having given priority to the claims of the firm. Such systems of priorities seem to me to have, among their significant features, the following.

(1) They may be quite complex, and involve sub-systems of priorities within a single main level of priority. It may be that, for me, family concerns have priority over business concerns; and also that, within the area of family concerns, matters affecting my children have priority over matters concerning Aunt Jemima, whs been living with us all these years.

(2) There is a distinction between a standing, relatively long-term system of priorities, and its application to *particular occasions*, with what might be thought of as divergences between the two. Even though my relations with my children have, *in general*, priority over my relations with Aunt Jemima, on a particular *occasion* I may accord priority to spending time with Aunt Jemima to get her out of one of her tantrums over taking my son to the zoo to see the hippopotami.

It seems to me that a further important feature of practical thinking, which plays its part in simplifying the handling of problems with which such thinking is concerned, is what I might call its 'revisionist' character (in a non-practical sense of that term). Our desires, and ascriptions of desirability, may be *relative* in more than one way. They may be 'desire-relative' in that my desiring A, or my regarding A as desirable, may be dependent on my desiring, or regarding as desirable, B; the desire for, or the desirability of, A may be parasitic on a desire for, or the desirability of, B. This is the familiar case of A's being desired, or desirable for the sake of B. But desires and desirabilities may be relative in another slightly less banal way, which

(initially) one might think of as 'fact-relativity'. They may be relative
to some actual or supposed prevailing situation; and, relative to such
prevailing situations, things may be desired or thought desirable
which would not normally be so regarded. A man who has been
sentenced to be hanged, drawn, and quartered may be relieved and
even delighted when he hears that the sentence has been changed
to beheading; and a man whose wealth runs into hundreds of
millions may be considerably upset if he loses a million or so on
a particular transaction. Indeed, sometimes, one is led to suspect
that the richer one is, the more one is liable to mind such decre-
ments; witness the story, no doubt apocryphal, that Paul Getty had
pay-telephones installed in his house for the use of his guests. The
phenomenon of 'fact-relativity' seems to reach at least to some extent
into the area of moral desirabilities. It can be used, I think, to provide a natural way of disposing of the Good Samaritan paradox;
and if one recalls the parable of the Prodigal Son, one may reflect
that what incensed the for so long blameless son was that there
should be all that junketing about a fact-relative desirability manifested by his errant brother; why should one get a party for *that*?

It perhaps fits in very well with these reflections that our practical thinking, or a great part of it, should be revisionist or incremental in character; that what very frequently happens is that
we find something in the prevailing situation (or the situation
anticipated as prevailing) which could do with improvement or
remove a blemish. We do not, normally, set to work to construct
a minor Utopia. It is notable that aversions play a particularly important role in incremental deliberations; and it is perhaps just that
(up to a point) the removal of objects of aversion should take precedence over the installation of objects of desire. If I have to do without something which I desire, the desired object is not (unless the
desire is extreme) constantly present in imagination to remind me
that I am doing without it; but if I have to do or have something
which I dislike, the object of aversion is present in reality, and so
difficult to escape. This revisionist kind of thinking seems to me
to extend from the loftiest problems (how to plan my life, which
becomes how to improve on the pattern which prevails) to the small-
est (how to arrange the furniture); and it extends also, at the next
move so to speak, to the projected improvements which I entertain in thought; I seek to improve on them; a master chess-player,

it is said, sees at once what would be a good move for him to make; all his thought is devoted to trying to find a *better* one.

When one looks at the matter a little more closely, one sees that 'fact-relative' desirability is really desirability relative to an anticipated, expected, or feared temporal extension of the actual state of affairs which prevails (an extension which is not necessarily identical with what prevails, but which will come about unless something is done about it). And looked at a little more closely still, such desires or desirabilities are seen to be essentially comparative; what we try for is thought of as better than the anticipated state which prompts us to try for it. This raises the large and difficult question, how far is desirability of its nature comparative? Is it just that the pundits have not yet given us a non-comparative concept of desirability, or is there something in the nature of desire, or in the use we want to make of the concept of desirability, which is a good reason why we cannot have, or should not have, a non-comparative concept? Or, perhaps, we do have one, which operates only in limited regions? Certainly we do not *have* to think in narrowly incremental ways, as is attested by those who seek to comfort us (or discomfort us) by getting us to count our blessings (or the reverse); by, for example, pointing out that being beheaded is not really so hot, or that, if you have 200 million left after a bad deal, you are not doing so badly. Are such comforters abandoning comparative desirability, or are they merely shifting the term of comparison? Do we find non-comparative desirability (perhaps among other regions) in moral regions? If we say that a man is honest, we are likely to mean that he is at least not less honest than the average; but we do not expect a man, who wants or tries to be honest, just to want or try to be *averagely* honest. Nor do we expect him to aspire to *supreme* or *perfect* honesty (that might be a trifle presumptuous). We do expect, perhaps, that he try to be as honest as he can, which may mean that we don't expect him to form aspirations with regard to a lifetime record of any sort for honesty, but we do expect him to try *on each occasion*, or limited bunch of occasions, to be impeccably honest on those occasions, even though we know (and he knows) that on *some* occasions at some times there will or may be lapses. If something like this interpretation be correct, it may correspond to a general feature of universals (non-propositional ends) of which one cannot have too much, a type of which certain moral universals are specimens; desirabilities in the case of such universals are, perhaps, not comparative. But these are unworked-out speculations.

To summarize briefly this rambling, hopefully somewhat diagnostic, and certainly unsystematic discussion. I have suggested, in a preliminary enquiry into practical acceptability which is other than technical acceptability:

(1) that practical thinking, which is not just means–end thinking, includes the determination or sharpening of antecedently indeterminate desires and intentions;

(2) that means–end thinking is involved in the process of such determination;

(3) that a certain sort of computational model may not be suitable;

(4) that systems of priorities, both general and tailored to occasions, are central;

(5) that much, though not perhaps all, of practical thinking is revisionist and comparative in character.

I turn now to a brief consideration of questions (A) and (B) which I distinguished earlier, and left on one side. These questions are:

(A) What is the nature of happiness?

(B) In what sense, and why, should I desire or aim at my own happiness?

I shall take them together.

First, question (B) seems to me to divide, on closer examination, into three further questions.

(1) Is there justification for the supposition that one *should*, other things being equal, voluntarily continue one's existence, rather than end it?

(2) (Given that the answer to (1) is 'yes'.) Is there justification for the idea that one *should* desire or seek to be happy?

(3) (Given that the answer to (2) is 'yes'.) Is there a way of justifying (evaluating favourably) the acceptance of some particular set of ends (as distinct from all other such sets) as constitutive of happiness (or of *my* happiness)?

The second and third questions, particularly the third, are closely related to, and likely to be dependent on, the *account* of happiness provided in answer to question (A); indeed, such an account might wholly or partly provide an answer to question (3), since "happiness" might turn out to be a value-paradigmatic term, the meaning of which dictates that to be happy is to have a combination of ends which (the combination) is valuable with respect to some particular purpose or point of view.

I shall say nothing about the first two questions; one or both of these would, I suspect, require a careful treatment of the idea of Final Causes, which so far I have not even mentioned. I will discuss the third question and question (A) in the next chapter.

5

Some Reflections about Ends and Happiness

I

The topic which I have chosen is one which eminently deserves a thorough, systematic, and fully theoretical treatment; such an approach would involve, I suspect, a careful analysis of the often subtly different kinds of state which may be denoted by the word 'want', together with a comprehensive examination of the role which different sorts of wanting play in the psychological equipment of rational (and non-rational) creatures. While I hope to touch on matters of this sort, I do not feel myself to be quite in a position to attempt an analysis of this kind, which would in any case be a very lengthy undertaking. So, to give direction to my discussion, and to keep it within tolerable limits, I shall relate it to some questions arising out of Aristotle's handling of this topic in the *Nicomachean Ethics*; such a procedure on my part may have the additional advantage of emphasizing the idea, in which I believe, that the proper habitat for such great works of the past as the *Nicomachean Ethics* is not the museums but the market-places of philosophy.

My initial Aristotelian question concerns two conditions which Aristotle supposes to have to be satisfied by whatever is to be recognized as being the good for man. At the beginning of *Nicomachean Ethics* I. 4, Aristotle notes that there is general agreement that the good for man is to be identified with *eudaemonia* (which may or may not be well rendered as 'happiness'), and that this in turn is to be identified with living well and with doing well; but remarks that there is large-scale disagreement with respect to any further and more informative specification of *eudaemonia*. In I. 7 he seeks to confirm the identification of the good for man with *eudaemonia* by specifying two features, maximal finality (unqualified finality) and self-sufficiency, which, supposedly, both are required of any-thing which is to qualify as the good for man, and are also satisfied by *eudaemonia*. 'Maximal finality' is defined as follows: "Now we call that which is in itself worthy of pursuit more final than that which is worthy of pursuit for the sake of something else, and that which is never desirable for the sake of something else more final than the things which are desirable both in themselves and for the sake of that other thing, and therefore we call final without qualification that which is always desirable in itself and never for the sake of something else." *Eudaemonia* seems (intuitively) to satisfy this condition; such things as honour, pleasure, reason, and virtue (the most popular candidates for identification with the good for man and with *eudaemonia*) are chosen indeed for themselves (they would be worthy of choice even if nothing resulted from them); but they are also chosen for the sake of *eudaemonia*, since "we judge that by means of them we shall be happy". *Eudaemonia*, however, is never chosen for the sake of anything other than itself.

After some preliminaries, the relevant sense of 'self-sufficiency' is defined thus: "The self-sufficient we now define as that which when isolated makes life desirable and lacking in nothing." *Eudaemonia*, again, appears to satisfy this condition too; and Aristotle adds the possibly important comment that *eudaemonia* is thought to be "the most desirable of all things, without being counted as one good thing among others". This remark might be taken to suggest that, in Aristotle's view, it is not merely *true* that the possession of *eudaemonia* cannot be improved upon by the addi-tion of any other good, but it is true because *eudaemonia* is a spe-cial *kind* of good, one which it would be inappropriate to rank alongside other goods.

This passage in *Nicomachean Ethics* raises in my mind several queries:

(1) It is, I suspect, normally assumed by commentators that Aristotle thinks of *eudaemonia* as being the *only* item which satisfies the condition of maximal finality. This uniqueness claim is not, however, explicitly made in the passage (nor, so far as I can recollect, elsewhere); nor is it clear to me that if it were made it

would be correct. Might it not be that, for example, lazing in the sun is desired, and is desirable, for its own sake, and yet is not something which is also desirable for the sake of something else, not even for the sake of happiness? If it should turn out that there is a distinction, within the class of things desirable for their own sake (I-desirables), between those which are also desirable for the sake of *eudaemonia* (H-desirables) and those which are not, then the further question arises whether there is any common feature which distinguishes items which are (directly) *H-desirable*, and, if so, what it is. This question will reappear later.

(2) Aristotle claims that honour, reason, pleasure, and virtue are all both *I-desirable* and *H-desirable*. But, at this stage in the *Nicomachean Ethics*, these are unelimited candidates for identification with *eudaemonia*; and, indeed, Aristotle himself later identifies, at least in a sort of way, a special version of one of them (metaphysical contemplation) with *eudaemonia*. Suppose that it were to be established that one of these candidates (say, honour) is successful. Would not Aristotle then be committed to holding that honour is both desirable for its own sake, and also desirable for the sake of something other than honour, namely, *eudaemonia*, that is, honour? It is not clear, moreover, that this prima facie inconsistency can be eliminated by an appeal to the non-extensionality of the context "——is desirable". For while the argument-pattern 'α is desirable for the sake of β, β is identical with γ; *so*, α is desirable for the sake of γ' may be invalid, it is by no means clear that the argument-pattern 'α is desirable for the sake of β, *necessarily* β is identical with γ; *so*, α is desirable for the sake of γ' is invalid. And, if it were true that *eudaemonia* is to be identified with honour, this would presumably be a non-contingent truth.

(3) Suppose the following: (*a*) playing golf and playing tennis are each I-desirables, (*b*) each is conducive to physical fitness, which is itself I-desirable, (*c*) that a daily round of golf and a daily couple of hours of tennis are each sufficient for peak physical fitness, and (if you like, for simplicity), (*d*) that there is no third route to physical fitness. Now, X and Y accept all these suppositions; X plays golf daily, and Y plays both golf and tennis daily. It seems difficult to deny, *first*, that it is quite conceivable that all of the sporting activities of these gentlemen are undertaken both for their own sake and also for the sake of physical fitness, and, *second*, that (*pro*

tanto) the life of Y is more desirable than the life of X, since Y has the value of playing tennis while X does not. The fact that in Y's life physical fitness is overdetermined does not seem to be a ground for denying that he pursues both golf and tennis for the sake of physical fitness; if we wished to deny this, it looks as if we could, in certain circumstances, be faced with the unanswerable question, "If he doesn't pursue each for the sake of physical fitness, then *which* one does he pursue for physical fitness?"

Let us now consider how close an analogy to this example we can construct if we search for one which replaces references to physical fitness by references to *eudaemonia*. We might suppose that X and Y have it in common that they have distinguished academic lives, satisfying family situations, and are healthy and prosperous; that they value, and rightly value, these aspects of their existences for their own sakes and also regard them as contributing to their *eudaemonia*. Each regards himself as a thoroughly happy man. But Y, unlike X, also composes poetry, an activity which he cares about and which he also thinks of as something which contributes to his *eudaemonia*; the time which Y devotes to poetic endeavour is spent by X pottering about the house doing nothing in particular. We now raise the question whether or not Y's life is more desirable than X's, on the grounds that it contains an I-desirable element, poetic composition, which X's life does not contain, and that there is no counterbalancing element present in X's life but absent in Y's.

One conceivable answer would be that Y's life is indeed more desirable than X's, since it contains an additional value, but that this fact is consistent with their being *equal* in respect of *eudaemonia*, in line with the supposition that each regards himself as thoroughly happy. If we give this answer we, in effect, reject the Aristotelian idea that *eudaemonia* is, in the appropriate sense, self-sufficient. There seems to me, however, to be good reason not to give this answer. Commentators have disagreed about the precise interpretation of the word "eudaemonia", but none, so far as I know, has suggested what I think of as much the most plausible conjecture; namely, that "eudaemonia" is to be understood as the name for that state or condition which one's good *daemon* would (if he could) ensure for one; and my good *daemon* is a being motivated, with respect to me, solely by concern for my well-being or happiness.

To change the idiom, "eudaemonia" is the general characterization of what a full-time and unhampered fairy godmother would secure for you. The identifications regarded by Aristotle as unexcitingly correct, of *eudaemonia* with doing well and with living well, now begin to look like necessary truths. If this interpretation of "eudaemonia" is correct (as I shall brazenly assume) then it would be quite impossible for Y's life to be more desirable than X's, though X and Y are equal in respect of *eudaemonia*; for this would amount to Y's being better off than X, though both are equally well-off.

Various other possible answers remain. It might be held that not only is Y's life more desirable than X's, but Y is more *eudaemon* (better off) than X. This idea preserves the proposed conceptual connection between *eudaemonia* and being well-off, and relies on the not wholly implausible principle that the addition of a value to a life enhances the value of that life (whatever, perhaps, the liver may think). One might think of such a principle, when more fully stated, as laying down or implying that any increase in the combined value of the H-desirable elements realized in a particular life is reflected, in a constant proportion, in an increase in the degree of happiness or well-being exemplified by that life; or, more cautiously, that the increase in happiness is not determined by a constant proportion, but rather in some manner analogous to the phenomenon of diminishing marginal utility. I am inclined to see the argument of this chapter as leading towards a discreet erosion of the idea that the degree of a particular person's happiness is the value of a function the arguments of which are measures of the particular H-desirables realized in that person's life, no matter what function is suggested; but at the present moment it will be sufficient to cast doubt on the acceptability of any of the crudest versions of this idea. To revert to the case of X and Y: it seems to me that when we speak of the desirability of X's life or of Y's life, the desirability of which we are speaking is the desirability of that life *from the point of view of the person whose life it is*; and that it is therefore counterintuitive to suppose that, for example, X who thinks of himself as "perfectly happy" and so not to be made either better off or more happy (though perhaps more accomplished) by an injection of poetry composition, should be making a misassessment of what his state of well-being would be if the composition of poetry were added to his occupation. Furthermore, if the pursuit of happiness is to be *the* proper end, or even *a* proper end, of living, to suppose that the added realization of a further H-desirable to a life automatically increases the happiness or well-being of the possessor of that life will involve a commitment to an ethical position which I, for one, find somewhat unattractive; one would be committed to advocating too unbridled an *eudae-monic* expansionism.

A more attractive position would be to suppose that we should invoke, with respect to the example under consideration, an analogue not of diminishing marginal utility, but of what might be called vanishing marginal utility; to suppose, that is, that X and Y are, or at least may be, equally well-off and equally happy even though Y's life contains an H-desirable element which is lacking in X's life; that at a certain point, so to speak, the bucket of happiness is filled, and no further inpouring of realized H-desirables has any effect on its contents. This position would be analogous to the view I adopted earlier with respect to the possible over-determination of physical fitness. Even should this position be correct, it must be recognized that the really interesting work still remains to be done; that would consist in the characterization of the conditions which determine whether the realization of a particular set of H-desirables is sufficient to fill the bucket.

The main result, then, of the discussion has been to raise two matters for exploration; *first*, the possibility of a distinction between items which are merely I-desirable and items which are not only I-desirable but also H-desirable; and, *second*, the possibility that the degree of happiness exemplified by a life may be overdetermined by the set of H-desirables realized in that life, together with the need to characterize the conditions which govern such overdetermination.

(4) Let us move in a different direction. I have already remarked that, with respect to the desirability-status of happiness and of the means thereto, Aristotle subscribed to two theses, with which I have no quarrel (or, at least, shall *voice* no quarrel).

(A) That some things are both I-desirable and H-desirable (are both ends in themselves and also means to happiness).
(B) That happiness, while desirable in itself, is not desirable for the sake of any further end.

I have suggested the possibility that a further thesis might be true (though I have not claimed that it is true), namely:

(C) That some things are I-desirable without being H-desirable (and, one might add, perhaps without being desirable for the sake of any further end, in which case happiness will not be the *only* item which is not desirable for the sake of any further end).

But there are two further as yet unmentioned theses which I am inclined to regard as being not only true, but also important: first,

(D) Any item which is *directly* H-desirable must be I-desirable.

And second,

(E) Happiness is attainable only via the realization of items which are I-desirable (and also of course H-desirable).

Thesis (D) would allow that an item could be *indirectly* H-desirable without being I-desirable; engaging in morning press-ups could be such an item, but only if it were desirable for the sake of (let us say) playing cricket well, which would plainly be itself an item which was both I-desirable and H-desirable. A thesis related to (D), namely, (D′). (An item can be directly conducive to the happiness of an individual x only if it is regarded by x as being I-desirable) seems to me *very likely* to be true; the question whether not only (D′) but (D) are true would depend on whether a man who misconceives (if that be possible) certain items as being I-desirable could properly be said to achieve happiness through the realization of those items. To take an extreme case, could a wicked man who pervertedly regards cheating others in an ingenious way as being I-desirable, and who delights in so doing, properly be said to be (*pro tanto*) achieving happiness? I think Aristotle would answer negatively, and I am *rather inclined* to side with him; but I recognize that there is much to debate. A consequence of thesis (D), if true, would be that there cannot be a happiness-pill (a pill the taking of which leads directly to happiness); there could be (and maybe there is) a pill which leads directly to "feeling good" or to euphoria; but these states would have to be distinguishable from happiness.

Thesis (E) would imply that happiness is essentially a *dependent* state; happiness cannot just happen; its realization is conditional upon the realization of one or more items which give rise to it. Happiness should be thought of adverbially; to be happy is, for some x, to x happily or with happiness. And reflection on the interchangeability or near-interchangeability of the ideas of happiness and of well-being would suggest that the adverbial in question is an *evaluation* adverbial.

The importance, for present purposes, of the two latest theses is to my mind that questions are now engendered about the idea that items which are chosen (or desirable) for the sake of happiness can be thought of as items which are chosen (or desirable) as *means* to happiness, at least if the means–end relation is conceived as it seems very frequently to be conceived in contemporary philosophy; if, that is, x is a means to y just in case the doing or producing of x designedly causes (generates, has as an effect) the occurrence of y. For, if items the realization of which give rise to happiness were items which could be, in the above sense, *means* to happiness, (*a*) it should be conceptually possible for happiness to arise otherwise than as a consequence of the occurrence of any such items, and (*b*) it seems too difficult to suppose that so non-scientific a condition as the possession of intrinsic desirability should be a necessary condition of an item's giving rise to happiness. In other words, theses (D) and (E) seem to preclude the idea that what directly gives rise to happiness can be, in the currently favoured sense, a *means* to happiness.

The issue which I have just raised is closely related to a scholarly issue which has recently divided Aristotelian commentators; battles have raged over the question whether Aristotle conceived of *eudaemonia* as a '*dominant*' or as an '*inclusive*' end. The terminology derives, I believe, from W. F. R. Hardie; but I cite a definition of the question which is given by Ackrill in a recent paper: "By 'an inclusive end' might be meant any end combining or including two or more values or activities or goods . . . By 'a dominant end' might be meant a *monolithic* end, an end consisting of just one valued activity or good."[1] One's initial reaction to this formulation may fall short of overwhelming enlightenment, among other things, perhaps, because the verb 'include' appears within

[1] J. L. Ackrill, *Aristotle on Eudaemonia* (Dawes Hicks Lecture; Oxford: Oxford University Press, 1974), 5.

the characterization of an inclusive end. I suspect, however, that this deficiency could be properly remedied only by a logico-metaphysical enquiry into the nature of the 'inclusion relation' (or, rather, the family of inclusion relations), which would go far beyond the limits of my present undertaking. But, to be less ambitious, let us, initially and provisionally, think of an inclusive end as being a *set* of ends. If happiness is in this sense an inclusive end, then we can account for some of the features displayed in the previous section. Happiness will be dependent on the realization of subordinate ends, provided that the set of ends constituting happiness may not be the empty set (a reasonable, if optimistic, assumption). Since the "happiness set" has as its elements I-desirables, what is desirable directly for the sake of happiness must be I-desirable. And if it should turn out to be the case, contrary perhaps to the direction of my argument in the last section, that the happiness set includes *all* I-desirables, then we should have difficulty in finding any end for the sake of which happiness would be desirable.

So far so good, perhaps; but so far may not really be very far at all. Some reservation about the treatment of *eudaemonia* as an inclusive end is hinted at by Ackrill:

It is not necessary to claim that Aristotle has made quite clear how there may be 'components' in the best life or how they may be interrelated. The very idea of constructing a compound end out of two or more independent ends may arouse suspicion. Is the compound to be thought of as a mere aggregate or as an organized system? If the former, the move to *eudaemonia* seems trivial—nor is it obvious that goods can be just added together. If the latter, if there is supposed to be a unifying plan, what is it?[2]

From these very pertinent questions, Ackrill detaches himself, on the grounds that his primary concern is with the exposition and not with the justification of Aristotle's thought. But we cannot avail ourselves of this rain check, and so the difficulties which Ackrill touches on must receive further exposure.

Let us suppose a next-to-impossible world W, in which there are just three I-desirables, which are also H-desirables, A, B, and C. If you like, you may think of these as being identical, respectively, with honour, wealth, and virtue. If, in general, happiness is

[2] Ibid. 10–11.

to be an inclusive end, happiness-in-W will have as its components
A, B, and C, and no others. Now one might be tempted to suppose that, since it is difficult or impossible to deny that to achieve
happiness-in-W it is necessary and also sufficient to realize A, to
realize B, and to realize C, anyone who wanted to realize A, wanted
to realize B, and wanted to realize C would *ipso facto* be someone
who wanted to achieve happiness-in-W. But there seems to me to
be a good case for regarding such an inference as invalid. To want
to achieve happiness-in-W *might* be equivalent to wanting to realize
A and to realize B and to realize C, or indeed to wanting A and
B and C; but there are relatively familiar reasons for allowing that,
with respect to a considerable range of psychological verbs (represented by 'ψ'), one cannot derive from a statement of the form
'x ψ's (that) A and x ψ's (that) B' a statement of the form 'x ψ's
(that) A and B'. For instance, it seems to me a plausible thesis that
there are circumstances in which we should want to say of someone that he believed that p and that he believed that q, without
being willing to allow that he believed that both p and q. The most
obvious cases for the application of the distinction would perhaps
be cases in which p and q are inconsistent; we can perhaps imagine someone of whom we should wish to say that he believed
that he was a grotesquely incompetent creature, and that he also
believed that he was a world-beater, without wishing to say of
him that he believed that he was both grotesquely incompetent
and a world-beater. Inconsistent beliefs are not, or are not necessarily, beliefs in inconsistencies. Whatever reasons there may be
for allowing that a man may believe that p and believe that q
without believing that p and q would, I suspect, be mirrored in
reasons for allowing that a man may want A and want B without
wanting both A and B; if I want a holiday in Rome, and also want
some headache pills, it does not seem to me that *ipso facto* I want
a holiday in Rome and some headache pills.

Moreover, even if we were to sanction the disputed inference,
it would not, I think, be correct to make the further supposition
that a man who wants A and B (simply as a consequence of wanting A and wanting B) would, or even could, want A (or want B)
for the sake of, or *with a view to*, realizing A and B. So even if,
in world W, a man could be said to want A and B and C, on the
strength of wanting each one of them, some further condition would

have to be fulfilled before we could say of him that he wanted each of them for the sake of realizing A and B and C, that is, for the sake of achieving happiness-in-W.

In an attempt to do justice to the idea that happiness should be treated as being an 'inclusive' end, let me put forward a modest proposal; not, perhaps, the only possible proposal, but one which may seem reasonably intuitive. Let us categorize, for present purposes, the I-desirables in world W as 'universals'. I propose that to want, severally, each of these I-desirables should be regarded as equivalent to wanting the *set* whose members are just those I-desirables, with the understanding that a set of universals is not itself a universal. So to want A, want B, and want C is equivalent to wanting the set whose members are A, B, and C ('the happiness-in-W set'). To want happiness-in-W requires satisfaction of the stronger condition of wanting A and B and C, which in turn is equivalent to wanting something which *is* a universal, namely, a compound universal in which are *included* just those universals which are *elements* of the happiness-in-W set. I shall not attempt to present a *necessary and sufficient* condition for the fulfilment of the stronger rather than merely of the weaker condition; but I shall suggest an important *sufficient* condition for this state of affairs. The condition is the following: for x to want the conjunction of the members of a set, rather than merely for him to want, severally, each member of the set, it is sufficient that his wanting, severally, each member of the set should be explained by (have as one of its explanations) the fact that there is an 'open' feature F which is believed by x to be exemplified by the set, and the realization of which is desired by x. By an *open* feature I mean a feature the specification of which does not require the complete enumeration of the items which exemplify it. To illustrate, a certain Oxford don at one time desired to secure for himself the teaching, in his subject, at the colleges of Somerville, St Hugh's, St Hilda's, Lady Margaret Hall, and St Anne's. (He failed, by two colleges.) This compound desire was based on the fact that the named colleges constituted the totality of women's colleges in Oxford, and he desired the realization of the open feature consisting in his teaching, in his subject, at all the women's colleges in Oxford. This sufficient condition is important in that it is, I think, fulfilled with respect to all compound desires which are *rational*, as distinct from arbitrary or crazy. There can be, of course, genuinely compound desires which are non-rational, and I shall not attempt to specify the condition which distinguishes them; but perhaps I do not need to, since I think we may take it as a postulate that, if a desire for happiness is a compound desire, it is a *rational* compound desire.

The proposal which I have made does, I think, conform to acceptable general principles for metaphysical construction. For it provides for the addition to an initially given category of items ('universals') of a special sub-category ('compound universals') which are counterparts of certain items which are not universals but rather sets of universals. It involves, so to speak, the conversion of certain non-universals into 'new' universals, and it seems reasonable to suppose that the purpose of this conversion is to bring these non-universals, in a simple and relatively elegant way, within the scope of laws which apply to universals. It must be understood that by 'laws' I am referring to theoretical generalities which belong to any of a variety of kinds of theory, including psychological, practical, and moral theories; so among such laws will be laws of various kinds relating to desires for ends and for means to ends.

If happiness is an inclusive end, and if, for it to be an inclusive end the desire for which is rational, there must be an open feature which is exemplified by the set of components of happiness, our next task is plainly to attempt to identify this feature. To further this venture I shall now examine, within the varieties of means–end relation, what is to my mind a particularly suggestive kind of case.

II

At the start of this section I shall offer a brief sketch of the varieties, or of some of the varieties, of means–end relation; this is a matter which is interesting in itself, which is largely neglected in contemporary philosophy, and which I am inclined to regard as an important bit of background in the present enquiry. I shall then consider a particular class of cases in our ordinary thinking about means and ends, which might be called cases of 'end-fixing', and which might provide an important modification to our consideration of the idea that happiness is an inclusive end.

I shall introduce the term 'is contributive to' as a general expression for what I have been calling 'means–end' relation, and I shall use the phrase 'is contributive in way w to' to refer, in a general way, to this or that particular specific form of the contributiveness relation. I shall, for convenience, assume that anyone who thinks of some state of affairs or action as being contributive to the realization of a certain universal would have in mind that specific form of contributiveness which would be appropriate to the particular case. We may now say, quite unstartlingly, that x wants to do A for the sake of B just in case x wants to do A because (1) x regards his doing A as something which would be contributive in way w to the realization of B, and (2) x wants B. That leaves us the only interesting task, namely, that of giving the range of specific relations one element in which will be picked out by the phrase 'contributive in way w', once A and B are specified.

The most obvious mode of contributiveness, indeed one which has too often been attended to to the exclusion of all others, is that of causal antecedence; x's contributing to y here consists in x's being the (or a) causal origin of y. But even within this mode there may be more complexity than meets the eye. The causal origin may be an *initiating* cause, which triggers the effect in the way in which flipping a switch sets off illumination in a light bulb; or it may be a *sustaining* cause, the continuation of which is required in order to maintain the effect in being. In either case, the effect may be either positive or negative; I may initiate a period of non-talking in Jones by knocking him cold, or sustain one by keeping my hand over his mouth. A further dimension, in respect of which examples of each variety of causal contributiveness may vary, is that of *conditionality*. Doing A may be desired as something which will, given the circumstances which obtain, unconditionally originate the realization of B, or as something which will do so *provided that* a certain possibility is fulfilled. A specially important subclass of cases of conditional causal contributiveness is the class of cases in which the relevant possibility consists in the desire or will of some agent, either the means-taker or someone else, that B should be realized; these are cases in which x wants to do A in order to *enable*, or to make it possible for, himself (or someone else) to achieve the realization of B; as when, for example, x puts a corkscrew in his pocket to enable him later, should be wish to do so, to open a bottle of wine.

But, for present purposes, the more interesting modes of contributiveness may well be those other than that of causal contributiveness. These include the following types.

(1) Specificatory contributiveness. To do A would, in the prevailing circumstances, be a specification of, or a way of, realizing B; it being understood that, for this mode of contributiveness, B is not to be a causal property, a property consisting in being such as to cause the realization of C, where C is some further property. A host's seating someone at his right-hand side at dinner may be a specification of treating him with respect; waving a Union Jack might be a way of showing loyalty to the Crown. In these cases, the particular action which exemplifies A is the same as the item which exemplifies B.

Two further modes involve relations of inclusion, of one or another of the types to which such relations may belong.

(2) To do A may contribute to the realization of B by *including* an item which realizes B. I may want to take a certain advertised cruise because it includes a visit to Naples.

(3) To do A may contribute to the realization of B by *being included* in an item which realizes B. Here we may distinguish more than one kind of case. A and B may be identical; I may, for example, be hospitable to someone today because I want to be hospitable to him throughout his visit to my town. In such a case the exemplification of B (hospitality) by the whole (my behaviour to him during the week) will depend on a certain distribution of exemplifications of B among the parts, such as my behaviour on particular days. We might call this kind of dependence "component-dependence". In other cases A and B are distinct, and in some of these (perhaps all) B cannot, if it is exemplified by the whole, also be exemplified by any part. These further cases subdivide in ways which are interesting but not germane to the present enquiry.

We are now in a position to handle, not quite as Aristotle did, a 'paradox' about happiness raised by Aristotle, which involves Solon's dictum "Call no man happy till he is dead". I give a simplified, but I hope not distorted, version of the 'paradoxical' line of argument. If we start by suggesting that happiness is the end for man, we shall have to modify this suggestion, replacing "happiness" by "happiness in a complete life". (Aristotle himself applies the qualification "in a complete life" not to happiness, but to what he gives as constituted of happiness, namely, activity of soul in accordance with excellence). For, plainly, a life which as a whole exemplifies happiness is preferable to one which does not. But since lifelong happiness can *only* be exemplified by a whole life, non-predictive knowledge that the end for man is realized with respect to a particular person is attainable only at the end of the person's life, and so not (except possibly at the time of his dying gasp) by the person himself. But this is paradoxical, since the end for man should be such that non-predictive knowledge of its realization is available to those who achieve its realization.

I suggest that we need to distinguish non-propositional, attributive ends, such as happiness, and propositional ends or objectives, such as that my life, as a whole, should be happy. Now it is not in fact clear that people do, or even should, desire lifelong happiness; it may be quite in order not to think about this as an objective. And, even if one should desire lifelong happiness, it is not clear that one should *aim* at it, that one should desire, and do, things for the sake of it. But let us waive these objections. The attainment of lifelong happiness, an objective, consists in the realization, in a whole life, of the attributive end happiness. This realization is component-dependent; it depends on a certain distribution of realizations of that same end in episodes or phases of that life. But *these* realizations are certainly non-predictively knowable by the person whose life it is. So, if we insist that to specify the end for man is to specify an attributive end and not an objective, then the 'paradox' disappears.

The special class of cases to which one might be tempted to apply the term 'end-fixing' may be approached in the following way. For any given mode of contributiveness, say causal contributiveness, the same final position, that x wants (intends, does) A as contributive to the realization of B, may be reached through more than one process of thought. In line with the canonical Aristotelian model, x may desire to realize B, then enquire what would lead to B, decide that doing A would lead to B, and so come to want, and to do, A. Alternatively, the possibility of doing A may come to his mind, he then enquires what doing A would lead to, sees that it would lead to B, which he wants, and so he comes to want, and perhaps do, A. I now ask whether there are cases in which the following conditions are met: (1) doing A is fixed or decided, not merely entertained as a possibility, in advance of the recognition of it as desirable with a view to B, and (2) that B is selected as an end, or as an end to be pursued on this occasion, at least partly because it is something which doing A will help to realize.

A variety of candidates, not necessarily good ones, come to mind. (1) A man who is wrecked on a desert island decides to use his stay there to pursue what is a new end for him, namely, the study of the local flora and fauna. Here doing A (spending time on the island) is fixed but not chosen; and the specific performances, which some might think were more properly regarded as means to the pursuit of this study, are not fixed in advance of the adoption of the end. (2) A man wants (without having a reason for so wanting) to move to a certain town; he is uncomfortable with irrational desires (or at least with this irrational desire), and so comes to want to make this move because the town has a specially salubrious climate. Here, it seems, the movement of thought cannot be fully conscious; we might say that *the* reason why he wants to move to a specially good climate is that such a desire would justify the desire or intention, which he already has, to move to the town in question; but one would baulk at describing this as being *his* reason for wanting to move to a good climate.

The example which interests me is the following. A tyrant has become severely displeased with one of his ministers, and to humiliate him assigns him to the task of organizing the disposal of the palace garbage, making clear that only a high degree of efficiency will save him from a more savage fate. The minister at first strives for efficiency merely in order to escape disaster; but later, seeing that thereby he can preserve his self-respect and frustrate the tyrant's plan to humiliate him, he begins to take pride in the efficient discharge of his duties, and so to be concerned about it for its own sake. Even so, when the tyrant is overthrown and the minister is relieved of his menial duties, he leaves them without regret in spite of having been intrinsically concerned about their discharge.

One might say of the minister that he efficiently discharged his office for its own sake in order to frustrate the tyrant; and this is clearly inadequately represented as his being interested in the efficient discharge of his office *both* for its own sake *and* for the sake of frustrating the tyrant, since he hoped to achieve the latter goal *by* an intrinsic concern with his office. It seems clear that *higher-order* desires are involved; the minister wants, for its own sake, to discharge his office efficiently, and he wants to want this because he wants, by so wanting, to frustrate the tyrant. Indeed, wanting to do A for the sake of B can plausibly be represented as having two interpretations. The first interpretation is invoked if we say that a man who does A for the sake of B (1) does A because he wants to do A and (2) wants to do A for the sake of B. Here wanting A for the sake of B involves thinking that A will lead to B. But we can conceive of wanting A for the sake of B (analogously with doing A for the sake of B) as something which is accounted for by wanting to want A for the sake of B; if so, we have the second interpretation, one which implies not thinking that A will help to realize B, but rather thinking that *wanting* A will help to realize B.

The impact of this discussion, on the question of the kind of end which happiness should be taken to be, will be that, if happiness is to be regarded as an inclusive end, the components may be not the realizations of certain ends, but rather the desires for those realizations. Wanting A for the sake of happiness should be given the second mode of interpretation specified above, one which involves thinking that wanting A is one of a set of items which collectively exhibit the open feature associated with happiness.

III

My enquiry has, I hope, so far given some grounds for the favourable consideration of three theses:

(1) happiness is an end for the sake of which certain I-desirables are desirable, but is to be regarded as an inclusive rather than a dominant end;

(2) for happiness to be a rational inclusive end, the set of its components must exemplify some particular open feature, yet to be determined; and

(3) the components of happiness may well be not universals or states of affairs the realization of which is desired for its own sake,

but rather the *desires* for such universals or states of affairs, in which case a desire for happiness will be a higher-order desire, a desire to have, and satisfy, a set of desires which exemplifies the relevant open feature.

At this point, we might be faced with a radical assault, which would run as follows. "Your whole line of enquiry consists in assuming that, when some item is desired, or desirable, for the sake of happiness, it is desired, or desirable, as a means to happiness, and in then raising, as the crucial question, what kind of an end happiness is, or what kind of means–end relation is involved. But the initial assumption is a mistake. To say of an item that it is desired for the sake of happiness should not be understood as implying that that item is desired as any kind of a means to anything. It should be understood rather as claiming that the item is desired (for its own sake) in a certain sort of way: 'for the sake of happiness' should be treated as a unitary adverbial, better heard, perhaps, as 'happiness-wise'. To desire something happiness-wise is to take the desire for it seriously in a certain sort of way, in particular to take the desire seriously as a guide for living, to have incorporated it in one's overall plan or system for the conduct of life. If one looks at the matter this way, one can see at once that it is conceivable that these should be I-desirables which are not H-desirables; for the question whether something which is desirable is intrinsically desirable, or whether its desirability derives from the desirability of something else, is plainly a different question from the question whether or not the desire for it is to be taken seriously in the planning and direction of one's life, that is, whether the item is H-desirable. One can, moreover, do justice to two further considerations which you have, so far, been ignoring: first, that what goes to make up happiness is relative to the individual whose happiness it is, a truth which is easily seen when it is recognized that what x desires (or should desire) happiness-wise may be quite different from what y so desires; and, second, that intuition is sympathetic to the admittedly vague idea that the decision that certain items are constitutive of one's happiness is not so much a matter of judgement or belief as a matter of *will*. One's happiness consists in what one *makes* it consist in, an idea which will be easily accommodated if 'for the sake of happiness' is understood in the way which I propose."

There is much in this (spirited yet thoughtful) oration towards which I am sympathetic and which I am prepared to regard as important; in particular, the idea of linking H-desirability with desires or concerns which enter into a system for the direction of one's life, and the suggestion that the acceptance of a system of ends as constituting happiness, or one's own happiness, is less a matter of belief or judgement than of will. But, despite these attractive features, and despite its air of simplifying iconoclasm, the position which is propounded can hardly be regarded as tenable. When looked at more closely, it can be seen to be just another form of subjectivism: what are ostensibly beliefs that particular items are conducive to happiness are represented as being in fact psychological states or attitudes, other than beliefs, with regard to these items; and it is vulnerable to variants of stock objections to subjectivist manœuvres. That in common speech and thought we have application for, and so need a philosophical account of, not only the idea of desiring things for the sake of happiness but, also, that of *being* happy (or well-off), is passed over; and should it turn out that the position under consideration has no account to offer of the latter idea, that would be not only paradoxical but also, quite likely, theoretically disastrous. For it would seem to be the case that the construction or adoption of a system of ends for the direction of life is something which can be done well or badly, or better or less well; that being so, there will be a demand for the specification of the criteria governing this area of evaluation; and it will be difficult to avoid the idea that the conditions characteristic of a *good* system of ends will be determined by the fact that the adoption of a system conforming to those conditions will lead, or is likely to lead, or other things being equal will lead, to the realization of happiness; to something, that is, which the approach under consideration might well not be able to accommodate.

So it begins to look as if we may be back where we were before the start of this latest discussion. But perhaps not quite; for, per-haps, something can be done with the notion of a set or system of ends which is suitable for the direction of life. The leading idea would be of a system which is maximally stable, one whose employment for the direction of life would be maximally conducive to its continued employment for that purpose, which would be maximally self-perpetuating. To put the matter another way, a system of ends would be stable to the extent to which, though not constitutionally immune from modification, it could accommodate changes of circumstances or vicissitudes which would impose modification upon other less stable systems. We might need to supplement the idea of stability by the idea of flexibility; a system will be flexible in so far as, should modifications be demanded, they are achievable by easy adjustment and evolution; flounderings, crises, and revolutions will be excluded or at a minimum. A succession of systems of ends within a person's consciousness could then be regarded as stages in the development of a single life-scheme, rather than as the replacement of one life-scheme by another. We might find it desirable also to incorporate into the working-out of these ideas a distinction, already foreshadowed, between happiness-in-general and happiness-for-an-individual. We might hope that it would be possible to present happiness-in-general as a system of possible ends which would be specified in highly general terms (since the specification must be arrived at in abstraction from the idiosyncrasies of particular persons and their circumstances), a system which would be determined either by its stability relative to stock vicissitudes in the human condition, or (as I suspect) in some other way; and we might further hope that happiness for an individual might lie in the possession, and operation for the guidance of life, of a system of ends which (*a*) would be a specific and personalized derivative, determined by that individual's character, abilities, and situations in the world, of the system constitutive of happiness in general; and (*b*) the adoption of which would be stable for that individual in his circumstances.

The idea that happiness might be fully, or at least partially, characterized in something like this kind of way would receive some support if we could show reason to suppose that features which could plausibly be regarded, or which indeed actually *have* been regarded, as characteristic of happiness, or at least of a satisfactory system for the guidance of life, are also features which are conducive to stability. I shall list some features for which, in this regard, the prospects seem good.

(1) *Feasibility*. An adopted system of ends should be workable; the more it should turn out that actions and performances dictated by the system cannot be successfully undertaken, the stronger are the grounds for modification of the system. A particular case of the operation of this feature lies in the demand that an agent should be equipped, by nature or by training, with the competencies needed for the effective prosecution of his system of ends.

(2) *Autonomy*. This feature is closely related to the preceding one. The less reliant one's system of ends is on aids the availability of which is not within one's control, particularly if it is within the control of others, the less dependent the system is on what Aristotle called "ektos choregia", the more stable, or the more securely stable, it will in general be. Unless one has firm guarantees, it is better not to have to rely on the availability of elaborate machinery or government grants.

(3) *Compatibility of component ends*. Initially, one might suppose that there are grounds for the modification of a system of ends in so far as the fulfilment of certain ends in the system thwarts the fulfilment of certain others. But I think we have to recognize that, characteristically, an end is such as to be realizable in varying degrees, and that it would be unrealistic to demand a system in which the realization of one end was never diminished by the realization of others. What we in fact may reasonably look for is a *harmony* of ends; the possibility, that is, with respect to competing ends, of finding an acceptable balance in the degrees of realization to be expected for each end. How such balances are to be determined is a large and difficult question, but their unavailability would prompt modification of the system. This feature looks like an analogue of consistency, which is commonly favoured as a feature of non-practical systems, though perhaps more by some people than by others, like Wittgenstein and Norman O. Brown.

(4) *Comprehensiveness*. (An analogue for completeness.) A system is comprehensive to the extent to which it yields decisions with respect to particular practical questions; the more undecidabilities, the less the comprehensiveness. To be more accurate, the comprehensiveness of a system varies directly with its capacity to yield answers to those practical questions which should be decided in the light of general principles. In ordinary circumstances it would, for example, be inappropriate to try to invoke one's life-scheme

to decide whether one should have beef or lamb for dinner tonight. Deficiency in comprehensiveness seems to legitimize modification. (5) *Supportiveness of component ends.* A system's stability will be increased if the pursuit of some ends enhances the pursuit of others. Such enhancement may arise in more than one way; for example, a man's dedication to mathematical studies might yield increased skill as a chess-player; or his devotion to his wife might inspire him to heightened endeavour in his business of selling encyclopaedias.

(6) *Simplicity.* A system's effectiveness as a guide to living will depend, in part, on how easy it is to determine its deliverances on particular questions. If it yields answers on practical questions, but these answers are difficult to discern, the system will be at a disadvantage when compared with another, whose greater simplicity makes its deliverances more accessible.

(7) *Agreeableness.* One form of agreeableness will, unless counteracted, automatically attach to the attainment of an object of desire, such attainment being routinely a source of satisfaction. The generation of satisfaction will, then, not provide an independent ground for preferring one system of ends to another. But other modes of agreeableness, such as being a source of delight, which are not routinely associated with the fulfilment of desire, could discriminate independently of other features relevant to such preferences, between one system and another. A system the operation of which is specially agreeable would be stable not only *vis-à-vis* rival systems, but also against the weakening effect of incontinence: a disturbing influence is more surely met by a principle in consort with a supporting attraction than by the principle alone.

However promising the signs may so far have seemed to be, I very much doubt whether the proposed characterization of happiness can be more than a partial characterization. *First*, there seem to be features which intuition would require that an optimal system of ends should exemplify, but which cannot be represented as promotive of stability. Many people would hold that, other things being equal, a person's system of ends should be such as to involve maximal development of his natural talents; and many would hold that, where this is possible, a system should provide scope for outstanding or distinctive personal achievement. If these views are

correct, it seems difficult to furnish for them a justifying connection with the ideas of stability and flexibility. *Second,* the
features associated with stability seem to be, even in combination,
insufficiently selective. All the listed features, except the last, seem
to be systemic in character; and difficulties seem to arise with respect
to them which are reminiscent of a stock objection to a familiar
form of the Coherence Theory of Truth. Proponents of the idea
that membership of a coherent and comprehensive system of
propositions is necessary and sufficient for being true are met with
the reply that a plurality of such systems, each inconsistent with
the others, is conceivable, and that, to eliminate from candidacy
for truth all but one member of such a plurality, it will be necessary to appeal to an extra-systematic condition, such as incorrig-
ibility or certification by observation. In somewhat similar style,
we can point to systems of ends which, so far as one can tell, might
be undifferentiated with respect to stability and the features associated therewith, including agreeableness, yet which intuitively
would be by no means equally approvable for the guidance of living; for example, such systems as might be espoused by a hermit,
by a monomaniacal stamp-collector, by an unwavering egotist, and
by a well-balanced, kindly country gentleman.

To resolve such difficulties, an extra-systematic condition seems
to be required, one which will differentiate ends or systems of
ends in respect of value. Here I would seek to explore a road not
entirely different from that taken by Aristotle. I would like to consider the possibility that the idea of happiness-in-general might
be determined by reference to the essential characteristics of a
human being (rational animal); the ends involved in the idea of
happiness-in-general would, perhaps, be the realization in abundance, in various forms specific to individual men, of those capacities
with which a creature-constructor would have to endow creatures
in order to make them maximally viable in human living conditions,
that is, in the widest manageable range of different environments.[3]

[3 The original lecture version of this chapter concluded with this sentence:
"But I have now almost exactly reached the beginning of the paper which, till
recently, you thought I was going to read to you tonight, on the derivability of
ethical principles. It is a pity that I have used up my time."]

Index